# *Praise for the first edition of* The Overnight Résumé:

"The best résumé book I've seen, because of its clear and concise style. And it provides a step-by-step plan to find the right job, not just a job. A real-world approach."

—Teri L. Bellamy, vice president of Human Resources, Bank of America

"It's a new approach . . . teaches you to think about the employer . . . tells you exactly what to do and why. It's the style I use myself."

—John Noble, associate director, Career Services, Harvard University

"Mr. Asher is expert in emphasizing strengths and camouflaging weaknesses while avoiding the potentially career-killing lie."

—*Dallas News*

"An overnight sensation . . . you'll have a winning resume before sunup."

—*Working Writers*

"Packed with original tips from a pro. We've seen dozens of books on the subject, and this one really stands out in a crowd."

—Kennedy Publications' *Job & Career Library*

"Asher offers brevity, clear thinking, and good sense. . . . His résumé for Ernie the alley cat is proof positive that a résumé can be created from virtually any background. Highly recommended."

—*Library Journal*

"With this book, you can create an effective, hard-hitting résumé in just one day. . . . This book is for any career-minded person."

—Woman Engineer

"The most practical, readable, and down-to-earth approach to writing résumés I've ever seen. . . . In my opinion, Donald Asher is among the very best in the industry. I think I've read everything he's written."

—Anne Follis, author of Power Pack Your Job Search

## *And praise from readers:*

"The best book ever written. The bible of bibles!"

—Pat Long, Birmingham, Alabama

"My response rate was a stellar 90 percent! I sent out 10 letters and received 9 phone calls. All I can say is thanks. And thanks again."

—Karen Chapman, Ardmore Pennsylvania

"I sent out four résumés and got three interviews. The first company that called me hired me."

—Lisa Bertschi, San Francisco, California

"Asher's books have allowed me to change careers midstream, from finance to high tech without missing a beat. His guides are truly career guides and will help you make the career move you need to stay challenged and excited about your working life."

—Eric Schwaab, Boston, Massachusetts

# The Overnight Résumé

SECOND EDITION

## Donald Asher

TEN SPEED PRESS
Berkeley, California

**Ten Speed Press**
P.O. Box 7123
Berkeley, California 94707
www.tenspeed.com

Distributed in Australia by Simon and Schuster Australia, in Canada by Ten Speed Press Canada, in New Zealand by Southern Publishers Group, in South Africa by Real Books, and in the United Kingdom and Europe by Airlift Books.

Cover design by Cale Burr
Interior design by Jeff Brandenburg, ImageComp

Library of Congress Cataloging-in-Publication Data
Asher, Donald
        The overnight résumé / Donald Asher
            p.        cm.
        ISBN 1-58008-041-3 (alk. paper)
        1. Résumés (Employment) I. Title
HF5383.A84 1999        98-54145
808'.06665—dc21


First printing this edition, 1999
Printed in Canada

1 2 3 4 5 6 7 8 9 10 — 03 02 01 00 99


Some portions of this book appeared in the *Wall Street Journal's National Business Employment Weekly* and *Managing Your Career* magazines. They are used here by permission of Dow Jones, Inc. Some forms and examples in this book are adapted from material in *Asher's Bible of Executive Résumés, From College to Career,* and *The Foolproof Job-Search Workbook.* They are used here by permission of Ten Speed Press.

## A Note from the Author

The only significant difference between people who do things and people who don't is exactly that. Pick up this book and do something to make your life better.

—*Donald Asher*
Asher Associates
San Francisco
(415) 543-7130

*To my staff over the years:* Kathy Priola, Kathleen Docherty, Penelope Bell, Robin Klayman, Patricia O'Keefe, Christine Lee, Joe Caffall, Rich Matheson, Frank Antonelli, Andrea Miskow, Leigh Hancock, Susan Hall, Lisa Lenker, Marsha Keeffer, Sharon McNally, Dave Soss, David Glober, Tia Woodward, and John Heed. Nobody ever had a better staff.

*To Lisabeth Bertschi,* for winning a $100 bet with such grace, even if it was a bittersweet win.

*To my clients,* who taught me all the best tricks.

Special thanks to Mary-Ellen Mort, e-search goddess and project director for JobSmart. Special thanks to Denise Rhiner from Reed College for her outstanding and above-and-beyond-the-call-of-duty research assistance. Special thanks to Stan Shpetner from Georgetown University for his research assistance. Special thanks to Rebecca Lemov from Yale University for her copyediting expertise, and to Wade Fox for the same services on the second edition. Special thanks, as always, to Mariah Bear, my executive editor, for her keen wit and patience. Thanks again to George Young for buying this book in the first place, and thanks for the first time to Kirsty Melville for seeking another edition. Thanks again to Kathleen Docherty, for taking care of my business. Special thanks to Prof. Walter Englert, Classics Department, Reed College, for his wonderfully salacious selections in Latin from Apuleius's *The Golden Ass.* The errors are all mine, but many, many people have contributed to this book. Thank you all.

# Contents

Preface    How to Use This Book . . . . . . . . . . . . . . . . . . . . . . . . . . . . . . vii

Chapter 1    Why You Need a Résumé . . . . . . . . . . . . . . . . . . . . . . . . . . 1

Chapter 2    What Your Résumé Can Do for You . . . . . . . . . . . . . . . . . 3

Chapter 3    The Rules of Résumé Writing . . . . . . . . . . . . . . . . . . . . . . . 5

Chapter 4    Résumé English Simplified . . . . . . . . . . . . . . . . . . . . . . . . . 7

Chapter 5    Writing Your Résumé: Style Overview . . . . . . . . . . . . . . . 11

Chapter 6    Writing Your Résumé: The One Thing You MUST Do First . . . . . 15

Chapter 7    Writing Your Résumé: Getting Started with the Heading . . . . . . . . 19

Chapter 8    Writing Your Résumé: Win or Lose in the First Ten Lines . . . . . . . 23

Chapter 9    Writing Your Résumé: Jobs and Dates . . . . . . . . . . . . . . . . 29

Chapter 10    Writing Your Résumé: Education and Additional Data . . . . . . . . 43

Chapter 11    Writing Your Résumé: Putting It Together . . . . . . . . . . . . . . . 51

Chapter 12    Special Styles, More Tricks . . . . . . . . . . . . . . . . . . . . . . . . . 77

Chapter 13    Scannable, Internet, and HTML Electronic Résumés . . . . . . . . . . 95

Chapter 14    Directory of Career-Oriented and Job-Search Web Sites . . . . . . . 103

Chapter 15    How to Get Interviews and Plan and Manage a Job Search . . . . . 115

Chapter 16    Cover Letters: Don't Write One Until You Read Chapter 15 . . . . 135

Chapter 17    Go for It! This Is Your Life . . . . . . . . . . . . . . . . . . . . . . . . . 149

Appendix    Annotated Bibliography of Career Books . . . . . . . . . . . . . . . 151

Index    . . . . . . . . . . . . . . . . . . . . . . . . . . . . . . . . . . . . . . . . . . 155

# Preface
# How to Use This Book

*Choose a job you love, and you will never have to work a day in your life.*

—Confucius

If you want to have your résumé ready by 9 A.M. tomorrow, skip the rest of this prologue, read only the parts of the book with a grey bar down the edge of the page, and get started right now. DO NOT SKIP CHAPTER 3, "The Rules of Résumé Writing."

This book makes several assumptions about you, the reader. In order to best evaluate whether the book can be of use to you, you need to know what they are.

The assumptions:

➤ You know what you want to do.

➤ You are intelligent.

➤ You can write a reasonable, straightforward sentence.

➤ You are motivated to create your own success.

What is **not** assumed:

➤ That you are a "writer" or a grammarian.

➤ That you have a secretary, a computer, or even a typewriter.

This book assumes that you do not need psychoanalysis or aptitude testing; what you do need is a résumé, and you need it fast. The problem with many of the books in the "get-a-job" genre is that they attempt to tell you how to discern what you want to do. The result is often a bit like swimming through quicksand, especially for the majority of us who know what it is we are after.

You may have picked up this book because a headhunter called you this afternoon or your favorite project got canceled or your boss yelled at you or because you just completed your doctorate in microbiology, but let us assume that what you need most is a résumé and a rational job-search strategy.

My experience is that most jobseekers are employed, do not have a week to read get-a-job books, and do know what their immediate objective is. If you are unsure, there are many good books on the subject. See the appendix for a quick overview of some of the best.

You must know what you want to do next to proceed. You will not succeed if you do not.

I assume that you are intelligent. It is a fascinating statistic that, in any given year, fully three quarters of Americans do not read one single book. If you are career-minded and you are reading this book, I am going to go ahead and assume that you do not need to be beaten over the head with a concept. Due to the brevity of this book, some very good points are made only once. It may be helpful to write in the book, take notes, and reread some parts as you go along.

Almost anybody can write a reasonable, straightforward sentence. You do not need to be a great writer, or even a good writer, to write a great résumé. Résumé writing is a formula that you are going to learn. This is business writing, not literature. Know your limitations and stay within them, and your résumé will come out fine.

Too much writing skill can actually be a detriment. One of the worst professional résumé writers I ever hired had a Ph.D. in English. He wrote beautiful, vivid sentences that painted a picture just as clearly as Michelangelo, but these sentences made horrid résumés. The reader's attention was drawn to the writer's literary embellishments, not to the candidate's accomplishments.

This book does not create motivation—it channels it. My assumption that you are motivated to create your own success is a fairly safe one, because you have procured what is obviously a *self*-help book. On the other hand, this book is designed to make highly efficient use of your motivation.

The process of writing your own résumé can be quite exhilarating. Distilling and recounting your accomplishments is intrinsically satisfying, but the impetus to begin must come from you.

**If you have read to here, pull out some paper or turn on your computer and keep going. You will have a résumé in no time!**

# Why You Need a Résumé 

## CHAPTER 1

The résumé is an integral part of the job-search process. Career books have been ringing the résumé's death knell off and on for over twenty years, but the résumé is even more popular now than ever before. I have seen good résumés for journeyman carpenters, for TV personalities, for CEOs, for management consultants, you name it. The résumé can be either a stumbling block or a springboard in anyone's job search.

In the simplest terms, here's why you need a résumé:

### Everyone Will Ask You for One.

Here's why you need it fast:

### You're Not the Only One They Will Ask.

This is particularly true of executive search consultants, also known as headhunters. Many people feel singled out when a headhunter calls them; they are convinced of the headhunter's genius and good taste. In fact, most good headhunters are on the phone all day long. They called someone else right before they called you and will call someone right after. If your lack of a résumé causes even a short delay, you are out of consideration.

**While Eugene's competitor was away from the room, a fire broke out in his attaché case.**

Another good reason to act fast is that speed creates a sense of urgency. Urgency creates momentum in the search process. Urgency and momentum make the hiring authority hire you instead of deciding to keep looking. More on this is in chapter 15, "How to Get Interviews and Plan and Manage a Job Search."

As you can probably tell, I am a big fan of résumés. Résumés have made great contributions to meritocracy and efficiency in American business. We no longer live in an economy where you can just go to work at Uncle Bob's gas station or Aunt Jane's conglomerate. Even if that is still done, it is no longer the model. You sell your skills to the highest bidder, presumably the one who can utilize those skills for the greatest return. And you use your résumé to sell those skills.

# What Your Résumé Can Do for You

A good résumé can do four things, each distinctly separate and distinctly important:

➤ Get the interview

➤ Structure the interview

➤ Remind the interviewer about you

➤ Justify the hiring decision to others

The biggest challenge your résumé will ever face is direct competition, winning the interview in the shoulder-to-shoulder battle with other résumés, many of which are from candidates with better qualifications than yours. Some glamour industries, such as airlines, receive in excess of one thousand unsolicited résumés *per day*. Following my guidelines, my clients have often gotten interviews and jobs at odds well in excess of one thousand to one.

Writing résumés that win interviews requires an understanding of what happens to your résumé when you send it to XYZ Corp. or post it on a Web site. If you send it to a company, it is usually screened by someone whose whole purpose in life is to decide who *not* to interview. Management time is valuable, so this first screening may be done by a clerk. Even if you are applying for a $90,000-a-year job, you must make it easy for this clerk, or your application will end up alongside yesterday's newspaper in the circular file. If you post your résumé on the Web, your clerk is a search engine, and you have to know how they work to get hits.

How to write your résumé is only one interview-winning key in this book. In chapters 15, "How to Get Interviews and Plan and Manage a Job Search," and 16, "Cover Letters: Don't Write One until You Read Chapter 15," I will show you how to avoid getting into screening situations in the first place.

Everybody knows that résumés are useful for getting interviews, but not everybody realizes the résumé's other, equally important, functions: It structures the interview process, reminds the interviewer of you after you are gone, and justifies the hiring decision to others.

Most interviewers will go right down your employment history, asking questions about each job. Your résumé should not tell the whole story; it should pique curiosity, begging for a clarifying question. (However, it should *not* be confusing or obtuse.)

Incidentally, you should take plenty of extra copies of your résumé to any interview. Your interviewer will often ask for one, and some interviewers ask for several as a ploy to get all of your copies away from you. Then they can test your memory. Have plenty of copies and pass this test.

After the interview, the résumé reminds the interviewer of what you have to offer. Even professional interviewers are strongly swayed by your written presentation. Research has shown that, after you are gone, the résumé can overwhelm the interviewer's memory of you in person. A candidate with a good written presentation will be remembered as articulate, well groomed, and intelligent; one with a poor written presentation will be remembered as unkempt, inarticulate, and ill prepared, *regardless of how the candidates actually performed in the interviews.* Few candidates realize how important this résumé function is.

The one major exception to the above occurs when an interviewer decides you are lying or grossly exaggerating. In this case all credibility is lost and your written presentation is discounted entirely. See the next chapter, "The Rules of Résumé Writing."

(If you interview people, be sure to prepare the same questions for every candidate and score each candidate's professionalism and preparedness immediately after she leaves the room. Then later, make yourself believe those scores.)

Finally, your résumé can justify the hiring decision to others. The hiring cycle can be months long, with many people involved. Everyone is afraid to make a mistake. If you are the wrong hire, it can be very difficult and expensive to get rid of you. There always are people higher up in the organization who rubber stamp your hire decision without ever meeting you. The better you look on paper, the more comfortable they are. Here the wrong résumé can undo every right thing about you.

Time after time candidates have come into my office and said something like "I don't need anything special; I've already got the job." My first thought is: Then why are they asking you for a résumé? Somebody is not yet fully satisfied, and that résumé had better live up to the rest of your presentation, or the whole deal could unravel.

As you are writing your résumé, keep in mind what you want it to do for you. If you understand what your goals are, what you want your résumé to accomplish, you will do a better job of achieving those goals.

Reprinted with permission.

# The Rules of Résumé Writing

## CHAPTER 3

The rules of résumé writing are simple:

➤ There are no rules that cannot be broken, with cause.

➤ Be careful of what you want, you may get it.

➤ Do *not* hold back.

➤ Do *not* tell a lie.

### RULE #1

**There are no absolutes in résumé writing.** In other words, every rule you have ever heard about résumés can be broken if you have a compelling reason.

### RULE #2

**Be careful of what you want, you may get it.** This proverb is as valid today as ever. Think about what you really want before you find yourself in some interview discussing it. More money, more power, and more responsibility are not always as much fun as you think, especially with the wrong company.

### RULE #3

**Do not hold back.** This is one of the few times in your life when blowing your own horn is *exactly* what you are supposed to do. If you are timid, force yourself to think of how your spouse or best friend might describe your skills and accomplishments.

If you state your skills and accomplishments well and accurately, you will increase your chances of getting a job that will maximize your potential. This is good for you, and it is good for society. So don't hold back.

### RULE #4

**Do not, I repeat, DO NOT tell a lie.** A blatant lie on your résumé is the biggest mistake you can make. Besides, it reveals a lack of creativity. The "problem" you feel compelled to lie about can be solved another way. Headhunters and companies check the basic facts on résumés, and there are even consulting firms whose sole job it is to do this. If you still are not convinced, consider the following.

I had a midlevel candidate who lied to me about a college degree, which I then put in his résumé. He had a great interview with the CEO. He had a great interview with the president. He thought he had the job. The president and the CEO agreed. They decided on $90,000 for a first-year salary, plus bonus and perks. He went to the director of human resources to fill out the papers and she said, "You know, I called your college and they have no record of you." The irony here is that neither the president nor the CEO was a college graduate. No one will hire a liar.

Then, I had a candidate who lied brazenly on her application, claiming a technical skill she did not have. To her credit, she learned the skill on her own in the first few weeks of work. *Seventeen years later* she got friendly with a coworker and bragged of her feat. You can guess the rest of the story. She got into a fight with her friend, and the friend wrote her up in a secret memo to human resources. When confronted, she admitted the transgression, thinking it irrelevant to her current position in management. She was summarily fired. Ironclad company policy. No one will retain a liar.

A lie can come back to haunt you after years and years and years. Even if it gets you hired, it's not worth it.

**There are no other rules.** It is absolutely *not* true that your résumé must be one page. Your résumé is first and foremost a business document. It should be long enough to achieve its objectives, and no longer. That is, it should be long enough to establish what you have to offer and short enough to leave the reader wanting to know more. For most candidates the résumé should not be longer than two pages, without a good reason (and there are many). It should have big enough print to be easily read. It should include roughly ten years of experience, unless more or less is to your benefit. All the important points should be introduced on the first page, if the résumé is more than one page. The information should be organized in order of interest to the targeted reader. It should be printed on white or off-white paper, unless you are in the creative end of one of the visual arts. These are all useful points, but they are far from rules.

# *Résumé English Simplified*

## CHAPTER 4

## Write a Letter to Your Sister for a First Draft

If you write a letter to your sister about your job accomplishments and then take out all the first-person pronouns and most of the helping and being verbs, all your tenses will be correct and your letter will be a great first draft of your résumé.

Put more technically: Résumés are written in the first person. The subject of most sentences will be *I*. Résumé English is the same as any other written English, but with the following removed: first-person pronouns, most articles, and many of the helping verbs. (True grammarians please forgive me for leaving out the 499 clarifying points. My goals are to edify without confusing and to get on to the writing part.)

One more time:

> ➤ Almost always delete the first-person pronouns. First-person pronouns are *I* and *we*.

> ➤ For a clipped and businesslike style, it is okay to delete most articles. Articles are *the, a,* and *an*.

> ➤ Delete most helping and being verbs. Helping verbs are *have, had, may, might,* etc. Being verbs are: *am, is, are, was, were, be, been,* and *being*.

Also, watch out for excessive capitalization, a literary style that literally went out about a hundred years ago. Proper nouns are capitalized, that is, nouns that refer to the one-and-only, unique-in-all-the-world instance of the thing named. You worked for the controller, in the accounting office, on the company's Bill Gates Litigation Task Force, on planet Earth. If in doubt, look the word up in a dictionary or check for more guidance under "capitalization" in a stylebook such as *The Chicago Manual of Style* or *The AP Stylebook*.

The classic secretary's manuals will instruct you to write out numbers ten and under, and to use Arabic numerals for numbers 11 and above.

For example, here is the letter to your sister:

> I have been part of the start-up management team for Rapido Architecture. I report to the president. I serve as the CFO. I participate in all strategic business planning. I have contributed to the phenomenal success of this company, helping it to grow from a small entrepreneurial firm to a $12 million international company with 100 employees and four offices. I directed the start-up of a subsidiary, Rapido Real Property Interests. I found a site and created a $40 million renovation project. I conducted a feasibility study for a proposed $150 million redevelopment of three properties in Washington, D.C.

Take out all first-person *pronouns,* and most *helping* and *being verbs,* and as many of the *articles* as possible:

> ~~I have been~~ part of the start-up management team for Rapido Architecture. ~~I~~ report to the president. ~~I~~ serve as the CFO. ~~I~~ participate in all strategic business planning. ~~I~~ have* contributed to the phenomenal success of this company, from ~~a~~ small entrepreneurial firm to ~~a~~ $12 million international company with 100 employees and four offices. ~~I~~ directed ~~the~~ start-up of a subsidiary, Rapido Real Property Interests. ~~I~~ found ~~a~~ site and created ~~a~~ $40 million renovation project. ~~I~~ conducted ~~a~~ feasibility study for ~~a~~ proposed $150 million redevelopment of three properties in Washington, D.C.

The result is a good first draft of your résumé, with a smooth and correct switch of tenses:

> Part of the start-up management team for Rapido Architecture. Report to the president. Serve as the CFO. Participate in all strategic business planning. Have contributed to the phenomenal success of this company, from small entrepreneurial firm to $12 million international company with 100 employees and four offices. Directed start-up of a subsidiary, Rapido Real Property Interests. Found site and created $40 million renovation project. Conducted feasibility study for proposed $150 million redevelopment of three properties in Washington, D.C.

Note that current and ongoing duties are in the present tense, and past projects and accomplishments are in the past tense. Then you will want to begin to edit your draft to spice it up:

> *Recruited* to be part of the start-up management team for Rapido Architecture. . . .

## Use Insiders' Language

Use insiders' language. Baseball players do not use the term "batting practice" among themselves; they say "BP." Similarly, the "players" in the financial world would seldom say "mergers and acquisitions" inside their own offices; they discuss "M&A activities." Use of insiders' language is a critical way of identifying that you are in fact an insider.

So, contrary to what other résumé books say on this issue, I encourage you to use jargon, acronyms, and abbreviations. Use them judiciously, but do use them. The test is simple: If everyone on the inside will know what you mean, go

"Strange how all six of your previous employers left the 'C' out of the word 'excellent.'"

---

*Note: I have left this helping verb as a bridge between prior present-tense duties and the next few statements in past tense

ahead; if the jargon might seem foreign to those on the inside, leave it out. Do not forget that your own company's most common jargon may be unintelligible outside your office walls. *That* is the type of jargon to avoid.

Some abbreviations are pretty common in most business settings. Here are a few examples of abbreviations and jargon that I think are usable in almost any résumé. They have the benefit of being efficient and can give your résumé a hard-driving feel: ROI, P&L, T&E, WIP, CFO, LOC or L/C, A/P, A/R, CPA, H/W or HW, S/W or SW, CAD, HRIS and the 5,324 common computer-related acronyms. If abbreviations are not familiar to you, then they are not insiders' language to you and you should not use them. If you know them and use them in a normal business setting, then feel free to put them in your résumé.

Finally, on the topic of acronyms, if you are a design engineer appointed to the Spacesuit Topographical Reconnaissance Inquiry Panel (STRIP), define it one time and thereafter call it STRIP.

There is more on résumé English in chapter 9, "Writing Your Résumé: Jobs and Dates," pp. 31–33, and chapter 13, "Scannable, Internet, and HTML Electronic Résumés," pp. 95–98.

### Third-Person Résumé

There is such a thing as a résumé in the third person. Sentences will read something like this: "Candidate possesses the highest standards of professional integrity. . . ." Headhunters popularized this style in writing about their clients, but I feel it is stilted at best. It is, however, a very good way to write a consultant's résumé. See chapter 12, "Special Styles, More Tricks," or, for more on consultant's résumés and headhunter styles, see my *Asher's Bible of Executive Résumés*.

To sum up: Tenses should be accurate, and you should be the subject of most sentences. **Write the first draft of your résumé as though it were a letter to your sister.** Avoid complex sentence constructions. Favor short, declarative sentences. If you follow these guidelines, your English will be fine.

# Writing Your Résumé: Style Overview

## CHAPTER 5

**The Two Major Styles of Résumés: Chronological and Functional**

Although there are hundreds of variations in résumé styles, there are two major and fairly incompatible families of résumé: the chronological and the functional. In short, the chronological states experience, jobs, and dates together, usually in reverse chronological order. The functional lumps skills or accomplishments together under headings such as "Management" or "Fundraising," then lists all the positions and employers at the bottom.

The first person to develop and use a functional résumé was undoubtedly a résumé genius. It is absolutely the most effective style for managing an unorthodox career, a complex work history, and other résumé "problems." However, anybody with a logical or coherent work history should use some version of the chronological style. There are two very good reasons for this: Functional résumés are difficult to write, and many employers hate them.

Why would an employer hate a résumé style? Because it is *too* good at hiding candidates' weaknesses. Consequently, candidates with problems gravitate to this style. Any experienced interviewer has wasted time interviewing unqualified applicants with intentionally deceptive functional résumés.

**"It's just about the cutest, cleverest resume I've ever seen, but the job's not about cute and clever."**

For example, under the "Management" heading a functional résumé may say:

> Supervised staff of 12. Gave daily assignments and monitored quality of work performance. Planned and executed comprehensive, geographically based marketing campaigns featuring entire product line.

**11**

Then under employment it may list:

**V.P., Marketing, XYZ Software Development Corp.**

But when it comes time to interview the candidate for head of a corporate marketing department, the interviewer discovers that the "staff of 12" were all youthful paper carriers, and the candidate was fourteen years old at the time. "Comprehensive, geographically based marketing campaigns featuring entire product line" meant knocking on doors and asking, "Would you like the paper daily, Sunday, or daily and Sunday?" XYZ Software Corp. was a garage-based pipe dream, staff of two (i.e., this candidate and, of course, the president of XYZ). This is what can happen when accomplishments are divorced from positions, dates, and employers.

From your own point of view as a résumé writer, functional résumés are difficult to get "just right"; it takes a wordsmith to excel in this style. I personally have the highest regard for the functional résumé, and we do write them occasionally in my office, but you are better off if you can sell yourself successfully with a chronological résumé.

The bulk of my background is with a fast-track management clientele, and they usually do have coherent backgrounds. This book concentrates on variations of the chronological style that are common, conservative, and successful for my clients. Almost any problem that would drive you to the functional style can be solved in the chronological style (special problems are addressed in each chapter focusing on résumé writing, and in the section "What to Do about Common Problems" beginning on p. 38 and "Gaps, Dates, and More Problems" on p. 41). If you feel you would prefer the functional style, and some qualified people do in spite of the above, then I suggest you read *The Damn Good Resume Guide,* by Yana Parker. It provides an excellent, well-written delineation of how to put one together.

## Control Your Reader's Eye

Your résumé is a design project as well as a writing project. The words have to look good together, regardless of what they say. As you write your résumé, you must also design it. It should look good at arm's length, and it should **control your reader's eye**. To accomplish this, use emphasis judiciously. Emphasizers that can help you control the reader's eye are bold type, italics, underlining, font size, and capitalization. The simplest word processing programs have all of these, but it wouldn't matter if you used a drafting pen to get the effect. Note: Do not mix too many different emphasizers on a page, as the result can be dizzying. Here is a sample table of descending emphasis:

**Pretty Big Bold Upper- & Lowercase**

<u>**BOLD ALL CAPS UNDERLINED**</u>

<u>**Upper- & Lowercase Bold Underlined**</u>

<u>REGULAR ALL CAPS UNDERLINED</u>

REGULAR ALL CAPS

SMALL CAPS

**Upper- & Lowercase Bold**

Extra Capitalization of Major Words in Headlines with Upper- & Lowercase Letters

Regular capitalization and lowercase letters

*Italics, only for book titles, foreign words, and* very *special cases*

You should note that underlining has fallen out of favor of late, as it does not fax well and confuses optical scanners. For more on scannable résumés, see chapter 13.

Save capitalization of major words for headings and titles, not for narrative passages. Excessive capitalization throughout résumés was popular all the way to the fifties, but in fact went out of standard English usage long ago. As a matter of fact, according to the stylebooks, even such titles as president, controller, general manager, and so on, should not be capitalized unless used as part of the title of a person's name, e.g., one would write "It was a 'gift' for President Clinton," but "It was a 'gift' for the president." Avoid capitalizing major nouns just for the fun of it.

When I want to control the eye of the reader, I will use emphasis out of the expected order. Note the following:

> The University of Arkansas, Fayetteville, Arkansas
>
> **B.S., Chemistry,** 1995

The reader's eye skips the school and concentrates on the degree and major. Compare with this:

> **STANFORD UNIVERSITY,** Stanford, California
>
> **B.A.,** Art History, 1995

See how different these two listings are? Although in many ways identical, the emphasizers control what the reader reads and its impact on her. Here is another sample, just for fun:

> **New York University,** New York, New York
>
> **B.S.** candidate, **Business Administration**

The reader sees what's in bold. Emphasizers are so effective that most readers scanning the listing above see a bachelor of science degree in business administration. This is *not* a lie, just good résumé design.

Be aware of the balance of the material on your page, and how it looks at arm's length. This is determined by word groupings, or listings, and the space between them. The mind loves a list of three, likes a list of two, and is not too happy with a list of more than four. You can be sure that no reader is going to be eager to read a résumé without significant white space.

This is a pretty listing:

> ➤ Nec mora, cum omnibus illis cibariis uasculis raptim remotis.
>
> ➤ Laciniis cunctis suis renundata crinibusque dissolutis ad.
>
> ➤ Hilarem lasciuiam in speciem Veneris, quae marinos.
>
> ➤ Fluctus subit, pulchre reformata, paulisper.

This is a pretty listing:

> ➤ Etiam glabellum feminal rosea palmula potius obumbrans de industria quam tegens uerecundia: proeliare, inquit, et fortiter.
>
> ➤ Proeliare, nec enim tibi cedam nec terga uortam; comminus in aspectum si uir es, derige et grassare nauiter et occide moriturus.

But very few readers will want to wade through a block of text more than five lines deep:

> Hodierna pugna non habet missionem. Haec simul dicens inscenso grabattulo super me sessim residens ac crebra subsiliens lubricisque gestibus mobilem spinam quatiens pendulae Veneris fructu me satiauit, usque dum lassis animis et marcidis artibus defatigati simul ambo corruimus inter mutuos amplexus animas hanhelantes. His et huius modi conluctationibus ad confinia lucis usque peruigiles egimus poculis interdum lassitudinem refouentes et libidinem incitantes et uoluptatem integrantes. Ad cuius noctis exemplar similes adstruximus alias plusculas, ad infinitum.

As a general rule, avoid using a bullet for *every single sentence* in the résumé. I call this the Teflon résumé: It reads fast but nothing sticks in the mind. It's popular at colleges, but I don't care for it even there. Bullets, yes; *every single line,* no. Also, I am definitely not a fan of putting headings in the middle of the page, a style popularized in the early eighties by electronic typewriters, which could center a line at the touch of a button. That was a long time ago, folks. We read in English from left to right, so put your headings on the left margin.

Again, while you write your résumé, design it as you go along. It is much more difficult to fix the design than it is to do it right the first time. And be very careful to be consistent! Your design makes a statement about you as a potential employee, about your detail skills, your marketing sense, and your ability to do a simple assignment.

**Control your reader's eye. Balance the look of your résumé on the page.**

## CHAPTER 6

# Writing Your Résumé: The One Thing You MUST Do First

*Reprinted by permission of Gail Machlis*

**You've indicated here that you would be uncomfortable accepting employment that might interfere with your nails.**

## What Type of Job Do You Want?

Back in the day before personal computers became as common as electric lights, a candidate would actually have her résumé typeset. Typesetting your résumé was a sign of stability. You knew who you were and what you had to offer. Today, it is a sign of rigidity and inflexibility. It makes a potential employer think that you are desperately mailing this résumé to every business in America with a known address. Times change, and so should you.

With word processors, you can *and should* prepare a unique résumé for every type of job you seek. That's right, you will construct a substantially different résumé for each substantially different job you target. Your résumé for office manager will be different than your résumé for executive assistant will be different than your résumé for departmental secretary. Your sales résumé will be different for selling Widgets™ than for selling Whatsits™, and different for selling solo than for selling as part of a team. Whether you are an executive or a college student, plan on reconsidering every word in your résumé *every time you use it.*

In order to write a great résumé quickly, you need to focus on your target. What type of job do you want this résumé to win for you? You can't write any résumé until you can answer this question. It's fine if you have a dozen targets right now, but which is the target you need to address first? Answer that question now, before continuing in the book.

Make a commitment now. Fill this out in ink:

---

The job I want this résumé to help me get is this:

    Job title:

    Industry:

Primary duties: _____

                 _____

                 _____

                 _____

                 _____

Title of the person I would typically report to: _____

---

Keep this target in mind as you work your way through the rest of the book and a great draft of your first résumé. You can make dozens more résumés later with different emphases, but this first one is for the job target you just specified. Stay focused!

## Point of View: Who Is This Thing for, Anyway?

Every employer has a sentence stenciled on the inside of her eyelids: "What can this candidate do for me?" Every time she blinks her eyes, she sees this sentence. It is a question you had better answer.

This is "point of view." *Her* point of view is the one you are going to think about as you write and design your résumé. A résumé is not a summary of your life, a chance to list accomplishments important to you, or a representation of your social and political values. It is an attempt to answer that question on the inside of the employer's eyelids: "What can this candidate do for me?"

As you write, you are going to adopt your employer's point of view. You are going to anticipate her concerns, guess what would excite her, and envision her motivations. You are going to get inside her head and pay attention.

Children cannot do this—cannot get outside of their own egos—but you can. You are an adult. You can foresee this employer reading your résumé. You can feel the paper, you can see her read, and you can feel her think. *You can adopt her point of view.*

I am going to ask you to adopt a point of view outside of yourself several times. Take it very seriously. It is the key to good writing of any kind, and it is the key to **great** résumés.

## The One Thing You MUST Do First

The one thing you must do first is *envision the ideal candidate for the job you want.* Forget about yourself entirely. Sit down, take out a fresh sheet of paper, and write down what you know about the ideal candidate for the job you want. This is one of the most important techniques you will learn in this book. If you will do this now, the rest of your project will flow like water down the mountain.

What **features, attributes, traits, skills,** and **strengths** would the ideal candidate possess? Close your eyes and "see" this ideal candidate at work. See her plan and execute. See her accomplish. See her make her company happy. As you do this, write down what you see immediately as it occurs to you.

As an exercise, let us do this for two positions: a sales representative and an accounting manager. Both positions are open at Acme Devices, a small manufacturing company with fifty-eight employees and just under $10 million in sales.

**Sales Representative.** The first thing I see is a smile, and it is a real smile, not a fake one. So, let's write, "friendly and outgoing personality." A related skill that comes to mind would be "never forgets a name or a face." Next, I see this sales rep working alone, so I might jot down, "able to work alone." Right away I think of "able to plan and execute a sales campaign independently," "able to develop a winning sales presentation from scratch." And I think of related administrative tasks that fall on those of us who work alone, so I write, "able to organize, track, and control a heavy work flow," and, "strong follow-through on details."

Then, I see this sales rep trying to crack a new account, and I think how hard it is to penetrate the screen around top executives, so I might write, "able to access the top management of targeted companies." Then, I start to think of how sophisticated the sale is to this level of client, and I see a sales rep who is smart and analytical, who "can develop sophisticated cost-benefit analyses showing the bottom-line advantages of Acme Devices."

Suddenly it occurs to me that I do not want to risk my new line of Wowie!™ devices on a newcomer to sales, so I want somebody with a "proven track record of success" or "demonstrated talent at opening new territories and launching new products." And I want repeat sales, too, so I write, "history of very high rates for repeat and referral business."

I am having a lot of fun with this hypothetical sales rep—we are sitting at a conference table adding up fat profits for the last quarter—when I suddenly start to think of things that could go wrong. Maybe this supertalented sales rep starts to look like an ego problem to me, so I jot down, "outstanding references from all former employers," and, "ability to fit into an organization and be productive immediately," which are different ways of saying that this rep is a "team player."

Finally, in addition to gross sales, I want organizational contributions from this sales rep. I want someone who "can train new sales representatives" and "can build new dealer/distributor networks" for Acme.

**Accounting Manager.** Again, close your eyes and see this ideal accounting manager. My own accounting manager is so trustworthy I let her run my business, so the first things I will write are "trustworthy" and "able to meet management objectives without direct supervision." Then I think, in rapid succession, "knows popular accounting and spreadsheet software," "able to learn and implement new applications from documentation alone," "able to design new statements, reports, and operating procedures as needed," and "able to plan and control work flow in a deadline environment."

Just to be sure we don't miss some technical skill, let's make a laundry list of talent for our ideal candidate: "general ledger, accounts payable, accounts receivable, credit, payroll, multistate payroll, commission accounting, cost accounting, fixed-asset accounting, cash report, quarterly and year-end report, annual profit-and-loss report, balance sheet, federal/state/local tax filings, you name it." And not only does he do these things himself, but he is "able to identify and develop talent in others," including "cross-training across the skill platform to eliminate work bottlenecks."

Reprinted with special permission of King Features Syndicate.

Since Acme is a small business, this accounting manager is also most likely the de facto chief financial officer. So the ideal accounting manager would be "able to serve as the company representative to banks, CPAs, the IRS, and vendors." Acme is probably run by a technician/founder, someone who is a good engineer and strategic decision maker, but who doesn't want to get bogged down in the details of business administration. So Acme would benefit from an accounting manager who could "support strategic decision making through timely access to financial and other data."

Finally, since we are dealing with the *ideal* candidate, I will even write, "never makes a mistake."

Take the time now to envision the ideal candidate for your next position. Again, *this has nothing to do with you.* Have an open mind, see the candidate in action, think the ideal candidate's thoughts, take the employer's point of view, and make a big list of **features, attributes, traits, skills,** and **strengths.**

Do not read further until you have done this. When you are satisfied that you have done your best, only then should you set aside your notes and turn to the next page.

# Writing Your Résumé: Getting Started with the Heading

## What You Need to Get Started

A pen and some paper. That's it.

If you have a computer, great, turn it on. If you have a typewriter, put some paper in it. Any word processing program will be fine. **Do not put obstacles in your way.** Let's go. Do each section in the order specified on this and the following pages. You'll have a résumé before you get up from your chair.

## The Heading

You may think this is a ridiculously obvious part of the résumé, but I do have a few significant points about it that seem to interest people when I lecture.

You need to start with your name, address, and at least one viable contact phone number. If your name is going to be difficult for the reader, consider adopting a nickname, as in this example:

Wei-Wen "Wendy" Lee

If your name is William Zebulon Harrison Styles, and everyone in the world knows you as Buddy Styles, you use a similar presentation:

William Z. H. "Buddy" Styles

However, if you live in the Northeast Corridor, Philadelphia-New York-Providence-Boston, nicknames are generally not listed on résumés, or indeed, on any written document. The protocol here is to wait until you are formally introduced to someone before asking them to call you by your nickname, although this is changing as regional differences are muted by worker migration.

At least let the reader know your gender, if nothing else. If your name doesn't reveal your gender, put a small title *after* your name, in parentheses, and in smaller type (if possible), to identify your gender:

Zbignew Brezinski (Mr.)

That old technique of just using your initials, which some women used in the seventies to disguise their gender, will backfire. Not knowing your gender just makes employers uncomfortable. Any employer will be reluctant to call you if they don't know your gender. Be practical.

**You absolutely must have a viable telephone number.** Very few employers will ever write to you, except to send a courtesy "No thanks." The employer will call, most often during the day. Usually they will call several other people as well. They will not keep calling *you* back if there is no answer, if your phone is busy all the time, or if your room-mate or your teenagers forget to write down your messages. It goes without saying that a cute tape machine recording is out and should be replaced by a more businesslike message giving your first and last name, at least. In my personal opinion, no one is seriously looking for a job who does not have a functioning telephone message system, either a tape machine or an automated service. Consider putting in a second home line or a home office line, and consider both rollover and message-on-busy features, so no one ever gets a busy signal when calling you. (A second line is also particularly useful for making outgoing calls, which are the key to a successful job search; see chapter 15, "How to Get Interviews and Plan and Manage a Job Search.") Call your telephone company for more information on all your options.

Put your office phone number on your résumé, if you can. That is a judgment call for you to make. The risk is that your current employer will discover you are looking for another position. Also, if you are leaving, or at risk of leaving, your office phone may be obsolete long before your job search is. The advantage is that headhunters and other companies can reach you at their convenience during the business day. It's your decision, but it's really important for people to be able to reach you by phone, and easily.

If your employer finds out you are looking for a new job, do not be ashamed of it. It is your right in the modern world. Ever since the mass restructurings that began in the late eighties, the covenant between employer and employee has fundamentally changed. You may even wish to sit down with your boss and engineer your own departure. On the other hand, if you do not think your company is so progressive, do not tell even your closest confidant about your considered departure. No news travels faster, not even that of an office affair.

In addition to your office phone, you may wish to list one or more of the following: fax line, voicemail, direct line to your desk, message number, or the like. If you are looking nationally or internationally, consider writing "24 hours" next to the number. If you are looking for work in a distant city, consider getting a toll-free line.

If any of this presents a problem, consider using one telephone line for all your job-search needs: a cell phone with an answering system backup and fax routing or remote reception capabilities. Make sure it is reliable and that no one ever gets a busy signal when they try to ring you. We are all approaching the "one-person, one-number" future, and a cell phone may be your best option if you travel, have kids, or live in more than one place.

Remember, the easier it is to contact you, the more likely it is you will be contacted.

**You *need* private e-mail for your job search.** Everybody needs e-mail. In many industries, e-mail is the preferred method of communicating. Recruiters now make most of their initial inquiries by e-mail. Not having e-mail implies you are technologically illiterate, a very bad sign in today's job market. *Do not use your office e-mail!* Recent court decisions have reaffirmed employers' property rights to your office e-mail; they literally own your e-mail. It is stored on their systems, and it belongs to them. When you hit "delete" on your computer, e-mail is not deleted at all. It is simply reassigned to a garbage file and can be mined at any later date until removed by a systems administrator. *Even then* it can be reconstituted by any halfway competent data specialist. You have to have your own private e-mail service provider. Unless you are forced by financial considerations, do not use a free e-mail service provider, and if you are in any technical field, be aware that some service providers are considered "cool" and others are considered best for complete idiots and newbies, so ask around before selecting a provider.

**Your mailing address is not as important,** except that it be understandable. Use a hyphen between a numbered street and a house number: 2201-16th Street. Do not use a post office box; it makes you look transient and unstable. If for any reason you do not like your address, rent one. Private mail services are inexpensive and give you what looks like an exclusive apartment address, such as 1400 Broadway, #212. Many employers do use addresses to estimate your commute, if they were to hire you. If they see a long, arduous commute, they may not call you, even if they really like your background.

Looking for work long distance? Unless you are an elite executive, you'll need to be invested in the local community. At least get a local address on your résumé. Use a friend's or relative's phone and address, or use a mail-forwarding service. You can also combine any local address with a toll-free telephone line or a remote-messaging or call-forwarding service. These services are not just for businesses anymore; they are inexpensive and easy to set up. Don't worry if your résumé shows a Chicago address and an employer based in Phoenix. You can explain your situation when they call, and believe me, you want them to call. Your local address shows you are serious about the community, and the employer will give you the same consideration as the other fine candidates available locally. At the middle management level and under, this technique has proved to be the clincher for my clients again and again.

Warning: Relatives can be notoriously unreliable, and mail-forwarding services can be glacial. Send yourself some mail and have a friend leave some messages, to test your communication channels.

Finally, now that you have spent so much attention to getting your heading just the way you want it, draw a line from margin to margin underneath it. That will control the reader's eye, and she will not even read it. A name and address by itself never got anyone a job, and you want your precious few seconds of screening to focus on what you have to offer.

**Note that many jobseekers use multiple addresses. Use any heading style you like. You have your paper and pen out, or your computer on, so design your heading now.**

---

**Jennifer Wilson Stone**

265 Nevada Avenue

Lake Tahoe, California 96150

voice/msg/fax: (916) 555-0239

jstone@nil.com

---

(The reader's eye is drawn here; résumé starts here . . .)

---

**KHAL N. KHORGIAN (MR.)**

knk@khorgian-inc.com

| *U.S.A. / permanent address:* | *U.K. address:* | *Swiss family address:* |
|---|---|---|
| 800 Pacific Heights Avenue | "The Cedar" | "Chalet Lisabeth" |
| Penthouse | 16 Copse Hill | Champ de Moulin |
| Laguna Beach, California 92651 | London SW20 ONL | 1296 Charmey |
| U.S.A. | England, U.K. | Switzerland |
| (714) 555-1381 | 44.81.568.6385 or 44.81.568.5816 | 41.29.75820 |

---

(The reader's eye is drawn here; résumé starts here . . .)

---

**M. R. "Missy" Menendez**

mm78@smu.edu

| *school address (until 6/2001)* | *permanent address* |
|---|---|
| 7845 Claiborne Way | 2731 Evergreen Court |
| Dallas, Texas 75246 | Shoreline, Washington 98155 |
| voice/msg: (214) 555-8545 | voice/msg: (206) 555-7313 |
| pager: (800) 555-8301 | fax (24 hrs): (206) 555-3857 |

---

(The reader's eye is drawn here; résumé starts here . . .)

# Writing Your Résumé: Win or Lose in the First Ten Lines

## CHAPTER 8

The hottest résumé style in use today is the profile style. It is what fast-track heavy hitters have been using for years to blow the competition out of the water. When a profile résumé is done right, it is a beautiful, flawless device, the perfect marriage of form and content. Most important of all, it is so effective it is scary.

Why does it work so well? Because it answers that all-important question—"What can this candidate do for me?"—in the first ten lines. Then it goes on to let the reader know that the candidate is genuine, not a faker, in the rest of the document.

Dilbert © United Feature Syndicate. Reprinted by permission.

The perfect career résumé has these three distinct parts: the heading, which you just wrote; the profile of what the candidate has to offer; and the chronological career history, both work and education, which is the proof that the profile is true. The profile works only because the proof is right below it. The profile and the chronological sections are a one-two knockout punch. In advertising parlance, you have the sizzle and the steak all in one place.

When you answer the all-important question in the first ten lines, you are doing everybody a very big favor:

➤ Your résumé will be sorted into the "yes" pile *without even being read.*

➤ Your résumé will be routed to the hiring authority *without even being read.*

➤ Whenever it is read, it will be reviewed with focused interest *right from the top.*

Obviously this saves everybody a lot of time; you are capitalizing on the fact that screeners take only seconds to screen résumés. You have actually made an asset out of the biggest problem most other résumés face.

### The Profile of a Winner

It is common knowledge that your résumé is an advertisement for you. In advertising, the profile is what is known as the "hook," the lines at the top of an advertisement that get you to read the copy underneath. There are car ads in national magazines with as many as five hundred words in them, about the same number as in a two-page executive résumé. All these ads have a hook at the top, e.g., "WOULD YOU DO THIS TO YOUR KIDS?" Otherwise, no one would ever read those five hundred words. It is the same with your résumé.

The names for a profile section may vary, but your heading could be any of the following:

➤ **PROFILE**

➤ **INTERESTS**

➤ **EXPERTISE**

➤ **STRENGTHS**

➤ **AREAS OF SKILL & KNOWLEDGE**

So how do you write this magic bullet? Simple. **First,** make a subheading that describes your functional area of expertise, such as: "Secretary / Administrative Assistant / Executive Assistant" or "Sales / Account Management." You can use a title, "Accounting Manager," but a functional subheading such as "Accounting Management" will give you more latitude. Remember, one company's "Controller" is another's "Accounting Manager" is another's "Chief Accountant." By using a broadly worded target, such as "Accounting Management," you will be in the running no matter what the company calls the position.

If you are interested in more than one type of job, you must choose which to focus on in this résumé (you can focus on the others in later versions). You must target your résumé from the top down; every single word is selected according to the following formula:

> **Put your information in order of interest to the targeted reader.**

For every distinctly different type of job you seek, you will need to have a distinctly different résumé.

So, you have your paper out, or your computer on, and you've finished your heading and drawn a line from margin to margin. You know what your target is. You are now trying to get the attention of a busy résumé screener in a matter of a second or two. Write your profile heading and your functional subheading now. Do not worry about doing this perfectly; you can always change it later.

Here's an example:

**EXPERTISE**

**ZEON Reliability Engineering**

**Next**, once you have selected your heading, answer the $64,000 question in the employer's mind: "What can this candidate do for me?" Go back to your notes on the ideal candidate, circle the skills and attributes that you actually have, and make them into a little paragraph or sequence of bulleted statements. Remember, you are the subject of each sentence: "I am able to . . ." "I have nine years of experience at . . ." "I have a solid grasp of . . ."

Do not claim skills that you do not have. If you cannot find the pencil you were just using, *please* do not claim you are "well organized and systematic." If you cannot balance your own checkbook, *please* do not claim to be "good with figures." If you are terrified to deal with strangers, *please* do not claim you have a "strong sales aptitude" or a "friendly, outgoing personality." The time you waste will not only be your own.

Make precise skills claims. Every grouch thinks he has a sense of humor, and every manager in business thinks he has "excellent written and oral communication skills." If you want to tell me about your communication skills, tell me that you have the "ability to design and deliver DOT-compliant driver safety training programs" or that you are "bilingual, French-English, including translating technical and legal documents into/out of either language." Prove you have technical, insiders' knowledge of the targeted industry. Avoid making a list of vague general business skills.

Remember, you are answering the question "What can this candidate do for me?" directly. You are listing **features, attributes, traits, skills,** and **strengths.** You may choose to include accomplishments or experience, but remember that experience alone is not what the employer wants to buy; she wants to buy the skills that should come with that experience. And remember, thirty-five years of experience is also "more than fifteen years of experience." Don't let anyone know you are ninety-five years old. And keep it short, less than ten lines.

Use every opportunity to slant your résumé to your future. You can write a profile that begins "Interest: Real Estate Sales," even if all your sales background is in career dresses—or vice versa. Be sure to differentiate *ability* from *experience.* "I have the ability to run a marathon" is a totally different statement from "I have experience running a marathon." (This is a full-fledged résumé trick; do not use it unless you really *can* run a marathon, if you get my point.)

Technical résumés work exactly like nontechnical résumés: They feature the candidate's skills and abilities right at the top, but they may include more tangential skills than nontechnical résumés. The trend is away from laundry lists of skills in dozens of different systems, applications, and platforms, and toward a claim of greater expertise in a few areas. However, if you are building a skillset for an Internet or scannable résumé, be sure to throw in the kitchen sink. (See chapter 13, "Scannable, Internet, and HTML Electronic Résumés," for more.)

Note that this heading and skills *profile* entirely replaces the old notion of an *objective.* You are offering your expertise, not acting as a supplicant for a position. My favorite résumé sin is an objective like the following: "Seeking a challenging and rewarding position with a progressive company with opportunity for professional growth and advancement." What does this mean, anyway? Not only is it vacuous, it is permeated with the wrong point of view. "Challenging and rewarding" for whom? "Progressive" according to whom? "Professional advancement" for whom? This does nothing to answer the employer's primary concern: "What can this candidate do for me?" Only use an

"Objective" heading when you really have little or no experience or skills to offer for the targeted position. In that case, objective may be your best choice.

One last thought: Do not be tempted to use the term *entry level* in your heading, or anywhere else on your résumé. It also is the wrong point of view. The job may be entry level to you, but to the hiring manager it is just another position that needs to be filled. Remember, at all levels you have skills to sell that the hiring manager wants to buy. Sell your skills; do not beg for a job.

— —

Write the rest of your profile now, drawing from your notes on the ideal candidate. To help you get started, I have pulled a few profiles as samples. Do not read ahead in the book. Finish your first draft of your profile now. Your goal is to get every major point into your profile that you want to convey to your potential employer. **Don't try to do this perfectly the first time!** Just draft a short paragraph modeled on one of the following examples. Try to get all your ideas out, and come back to your profile after you have written the rest of your résumé.

## Samples

---

### SKILLS

#### Office & Administrative Management

Ability to prioritize, delegate, and control administrative work flow to manage office or entire business. Skills encompass hiring, training, and supervision of support staff; design and implementation of policies and procedures; in-house accounting through trial balance; customer and public relations; liaison to banks, CPAs, and vendors; and support to strategic decision-making through timely access to financial and other data.

---

### EXPERTISE

#### Hospitality IT — Installation, Training, Support

- Experience includes conversion planning, business analysis, installation/implementation, diagnostics and troubleshooting, user training, telephone consulting, follow-up support.
- IBM ST/99 & ST/100, NCR 3822, Xeta, Northern Telecom SL10, Spectradyne, Teletron Energy, Honeywell, Extel Comexpert, IBM Life Systems Controller.
- Hospitality Data Control, SSI & Utilities, NCR FSS, Tel-Trak X.37 & X.11, IHC Global Reservations, Delphi Sales & Catering Systems, Acom Bookkeeper, Chouinard & Myhre P/R, ATS, and most other common applications.
- Available for 100 percent travel and/or relocation as needed.
- Proficient in Spanish; basic French, Japanese.

## PROFILE

### Registered Dental Hygienist

Stable and reliable, three years with current doctor, five years with prior doctor. Professional orientation is toward preventive treatment, periodontal maintenance, and patient education. Friendly, good with patients. Also experienced in office administration duties. Excellent recommendations from all doctors.

## EXPERTISE

### Retail & Commercial Real Estate — Acquisition, Planning, Development

Strengths include cash-flow projections, valuation forecasting, and financial and economic analysis of real estate development projects and investment assets, as well as presentations, negotiations, management, and oversight. Experience with both retail and commercial projects in the $10 million to $150 million range.

## PROFESSION

### Consultant to the Mortgage Banking Industry

*Strengths:*
- Systems & Operations Conversions & Mergers
- Reconstruction of Records, Loan Transactions & Histories
- Operational Reviews, M&A Due Diligence, Expert Witnessing

## SKILLSET

**Network Controller** with wide range of other telecomputing/data telecom experience. Effective combination of technical and communication skills.

| | |
|---|---|
| **Hardware:** | AT&T Dataport II |
| | CODEX |
| | General DataCom |
| | TRS XF 372.X, 327.X, 712.X |
| **Software:** | NCCS, NPDA, VTEX, NRS, JTCL |
| | MRI/XA, TSI/ISPL, MR/XLNT, MRI/SCRIBE |
| | NETVIEW REAL, NPO |
| **Specialist:** | NEX SNA network installation and maintenance. |
| | Some experience in network design. |

**EXPERTISE**

**Sales of Floor Coverings** (wholesale and to-the-trade)

- 16 years in soft goods/4 years in hard goods.
- 20 years of representation to architects and designers.
- Background includes high-tech/commercial/industrial applications.
- **Proven performer** with **sales records** on behalf of every employer.

---

**PROFILE**

**Clinical Psychologist,** State of Louisiana, with expertise in the following areas:

- Business, Careers, EAP, Organizational Behavior
- Psychotic/Severely Disturbed
- Alcohol & Substance Abuse
- HIV & AIDS Issues
- Family & Community Services
- Testing & Diagnostics

# Writing Your Résumé: Jobs and Dates

## CHAPTER 9

## Education or Experience First?

If the profile is the most important part of your résumé, what goes immediately beneath it is the second most important. You have two choices: education or experience. Education goes first if you have a brand-name education and you want to feature it; you are a medical doctor, a scientist, or a college professor; or your education is your best qualification. Otherwise, experience comes before education. If you choose to list your education first, skip to the next chapter, "Education and Additional Data," do your education first, then come back to list experience later. Either way, you can always switch it later. Remember the simple rule: **Put your information in order of interest to the targeted reader.**

## Experience

Before you even start, you must know that this section can include part-time experience, paid or unpaid internships, volunteer experience, temporary positions, and sometimes even experience gained in a classroom setting. Those entering or reentering the job market and those seeking to engineer a career transition will find this point of tremendous benefit. Most of us have job experience, but if it will bolster your candidacy, consider including some of these other experiences as well as, or even *instead of,* your primary job experience.

The following are all possible headings for this section. Choose one and write it onto your résumé *now*. Remember, this is just the first draft. Don't worry about doing it perfectly; just do it now.

- ➤ **EXPERIENCE**
- ➤ **EMPLOYMENT**
- ➤ **HISTORY**
- ➤ **PROFESSIONAL HISTORY**
- ➤ **EXPERIENCE HIGHLIGHTS**

Your job subheadings underneath should include name of company, title, city, and date. Here's just one example:

ACME DOGCATCHING SUPPLIES       Chicago, IL
**Assistant Export Manager**               2000–2003

If you are terrified your current employer will find out you are seeking employment, you can disguise the name of the company by giving a descriptive title, e.g., "A Major Reinsurance Brokerage" or "An A-V Rated Law Firm." This type of fear, however, is usually not impressive to future employers.

Dates are generally listed year to year, although students may list employment as "Summer 2000" or "Fall 2001." Listing the months you worked is just too much information that does nothing to sell you. Deemphasize the dates by putting them toward the right margin. If seniority is your greatest asset, you are looking for work in the wrong decade. That style of putting the dates down the left margin was popular in the fifties. **Never fudge your dates of employment,** as it is extremely easy for an employer to verify your dates of employment. If you want to learn how to overcome special problems, see chapter 12, "Special Styles, More Tricks."

Do not include street addresses, names of supervisors, contact telephone numbers, or other extraneous data.

Control your reader's eye! Be stingy with your use of bold as an emphasizer. Human résumé screeners will read anything written in bold, so don't bold dates, cities, or other boring stuff. You do not want your reader to get bored before she even finds out what a great job you did.

Leave cities out if they show you've moved all over the country recently or that most of your experience is in other countries, or if they present any other problem.

Always list your title accurately, as this is also extremely easy for a prospective employer to verify. If your real title is boring, misleading, or nondescriptive, you may use a functional title, but even then it is a good idea to list your official title in parenthesis. Here is an example:

**Laboratory Manager** (Senior Technician IV)

Remember, don't bold the boring part.

If your title was an old gender-based designator like *mailman* or *fireman* or *waitress*, be sure to update your title to *postal carrier* or *firefighter* or *food server*. This is one type of title change you should perform in spite of what your original, "official" title was.

You'll most likely be listing jobs in reverse chronological order, which means starting with your current or most recent position, and going backwards in time from there. You can also divide your experience into categories, such as "Related Experience" and "Additional Experience," or in topical groupings such as "Sales Experience" and "General Management Experience." You know the formula governing these kinds of decisions: **Put the information in the order of interest to your targeted reader.** Some of the résumé examples later in the book are organized this way.

To create a compelling résumé, your experience listing must feature **scope of authority** and **accomplishments** more than routine duties or responsibilities. Listing routine duties and responsibilities might win a support position, but to compete for a management position you had better describe some solid, specific accomplishments.

Take out a sheet of scrap paper and take a few notes on your current or most recent position. First, map out your scope of authority, then list some accomplishments. After you have a list, you can rank your accomplishments and decide what you want to include on your résumé.

**Scope of authority** is composed of your title (already listed) and the title of the person to whom you report directly; the size of the company, product line, or division in which you work, measured *in dollars* if possible; the size of the product line, division, budgets, or whatever you are in charge of, *in dollars* if possible; the industry you are in, the technologies you use to accomplish your work; and the number of people you supervise and their titles and functions.

Prospective employers need a picture of where you worked in their mind as they read about your background. If it is not obvious, you may need to typify or otherwise depict the company you worked for, as part of your scope statement, for example: "Loran Systems is a $21 million manufacturer of automotive aftermarket products with production plants in Ohio, Indiana, Mexico, and Ireland."

Your salary is also very much a part of the scope of your job but is never to be listed on your résumé. (See discussions in chapters 15, "How to Get Interviews and Plan and Manage a Job Search," and 16, "Cover Letters," for how to respond to requests for salary history.)

**Quantify everything.** Provide the exact number. It is a point of psychology that more people will believe an exact figure than a rounded figure. A résumé is probably one of the only places in the known universe where $9.65 million is greater than $10 million. Exactitude makes the reader feel comfortable with your skills claims and believe in your experience.

Every time you specify a figure, you increase the verifiability of your résumé. To a seasoned résumé reader, "supervised staff" has a slippery feel. On the other hand, "supervised 3 project engineers (team leaders), 17 design and mechanical engineers, and 23 drafting and technical support personnel" gives the reader a lot of confidence in the truth of your presentation.

The old rule from secretarial school was to spell out numbers one through ten, and use Arabic numerals for 11 and over. In a résumé, however, using 2, 3, 4, and so on makes for a good, businesslike read. I prefer "$350,000" to "$350K"; "$350,000,000" is very impressive written out fully, but it is a bit pretentious if everyone in your field would have written "$350MM" or "$350 million." Use your own judgment. Incidentally, on international résumés, "US$350 million" means "350 million United States dollars," a rather important distinction.

*On your scrap paper,* write a description of the scope of your job *now*.

**Accomplishments** are everything you did right. Throw away your position description and your flowcharts and let the reader know what you did *above and beyond* the minimum requirements. Your accomplishments section can include problems you solved, special projects, special assignments, training, travel, commendations, awards, and honors— anything that makes you special compared to all the other people ever to hold your title.

Ideally, you want to quantify contributions to the bottom line, even if your immediate task seemed far from financial. Perhaps you are a programmer who created an asset-tracking application that allowed a 5 percent reduction in production materials owned by the company. If the company owned $100 million dollars in materials, you can report that you "saved the company $5,000,000" with your application.

Even if you are a janitor, you should be able to report *and quantify* your contributions. Think like a manager. What do they care about? Here's an example: "Requisitioned 12-inch broom to replace 10-inch broom, creating 20 percent increase in efficiency in sweeping operations." Get it?

The classic formula for accomplishment is PROBLEM → SOLUTION → RESULT, hopefully with a dollar value on the result. In practice, however, you can list résumé accomplishments in thousands of different forms. Think, be creative, and be brief.

Explore different ways to represent the same basic fact. You can compare your performance to currently employed colleagues, to people in other departments, to prior employees, to people at other companies, in comparison to plan, and so on, virtually ad infinitum. Let us suppose you are writing this résumé because you just got fired. You were fired for lack of sales, because you only sold $1,000 worth of sackbuts (a type of trombone). But wait, the account executive before you was fired, too, after having sold only $500 worth. Let's face it, sackbuts are not very popular. Looks to me like you can say *in all honesty:* "Achieved 100 percent increase in sales for the territory, over prior sales rep." Never tell a lie, but it is your job to tell the best side of the truth.

## Search for the Superlative

Search for the superlative! I cannot emphasize this enough. You are the "first," "only," "most," or "best" something. I guarantee it. Be creative. Here are some superlatives:

➤ Top producer company-wide, out of over 100 full-time sales professionals.

➤ Ranked #1 sales rep in the region for Wowie!™ Widgets product line.

➤ First account executive in the nation to sign an order for the new Wampum!™ widget.

➤ Managed the fastest growing franchise in the chain.

➤ Merchandised the most profitable line in the company.

➤ Had the lowest error rate in the department.

And so on . . .

Observe the following transitions, each better than the last:

*Accomplishment:*
• Traveled to Boston for client meeting.

*Accomplishment:*
• Traveled to Boston with senior management for client meeting.

*Accomplishment:*
• Selected to travel to Boston with senior management for client meeting.

*Accomplishment:*
• Only intern selected to travel to Boston with senior management for client meeting.

Be sure to include intangible accomplishments. I consider a tangible accomplishment one that is figure based and that can be verified rather easily, e.g., "Increased sales by 38 percent in first 6 months on the job." An intangible accomplishment is not figure based and is usually a little harder to verify. Here are some examples of intangible accomplishments:

➤ Increased staff morale and reduced turnover.

➤ Improved the image of the product and the company.

➤ Saved several "shaky" accounts and improved account loyalty.

➤ Contributed improvements to record-keeping systems and overall office efficiency.

In all cases, do not be boring! Be excited about yourself! Use hard-driving language! **Start every sentence with an action verb.** "Handled" is a ho-hum verb, but "orchestrated" is a vivid, thought- and image-provoking verb. Although your résumé should not read like a war novel, use evocative verbs whenever possible.

---

### Effective Résumé Verbs

| | | | | | |
|---|---|---|---|---|---|
| Create | Implement | Schedule | Install | Administer | Attain |
| Design | Revise | Motivate | Analyze | Oversee | Evaluate |
| Manage | Reorganize | Coordinate | Prepare | Guide | Streamline |
| Supervise | Troubleshoot | Act as liaison* | Teach | Execute | Maximize |
| Direct | Overhaul | Select | Promote | Conduct | Facilitate |
| Establish | Resolve | Compile | Increase | Provide | Contribute |
| Plan | Initiate | Produce | Test | Generate | Consolidate |
| Devise | Originate | Ensure** | Start | Advise | Utilize |
| Organize | Train | Reconcile | Orchestrate | Develop | Negotiate |

*\*Liaise* as a verb did finally make some dictionaries, but it is an odious back-formation from the noun *liaison*, and I just cannot force myself to use it.

\*\*More exact than *insure*.

---

There is no magic to any of these verbs. You should use words you are comfortable with, but if you get stuck, just browse through this list. Sentence structures you should avoid, however, are "responsible for . . ." and "duties included . . ." These structures can almost always be replaced by more active and dynamic statements.

On your scrap paper, write up your accomplishments *now*. Be sure to quantify wherever possible, and be sure to include intangible accomplishments when pertinent. Start each sentence with a verb and use hard-driving language.

Do not read further until you have at least written up the accomplishments of your current or last position.

### Putting Scope and Accomplishments Together into Job Listings

Now you have all the components of a job listing: the company, your title, the scope of your job, and your accomplishments. Each job listing on your résumé should stack these components according to this formula:

As you construct the job listings for the draft of your résumé, you must decide what to include from your raw notes. This process also has a formula: **Throw out the obvious, then rank the rest in order of appeal to your reader.**

Remember your reader? Close your eyes and see that reader, someone able to give you the job you want. See that sentence on the inside of her eyelids, "What can this candidate do for me?" See her reading your list of points for scope. See what she will view as obvious and skip it. See what she will be most impressed by or interested in and feature each point in order of greatest impact. Do the same for your accomplishments.

Obviously, the order in which you put things is up to you. You are not bound by the FDA to list your ingredients by order of weight or volume. If you spent 10 percent of your time answering the phones in your last office job and you are applying for a job as a receptionist, you had better list phones first and go on to typing and filing later. You know the "ingredients rule" for résumés: **Put your information in order of interest to the targeted reader.**

Focus your past to relate to your future. For example, look at these two very different ways to present the exact same job:

A secretary seeking a job as receptionist:

> Mutual Benevolent of Omaha, Omaha, Nebraska, 2001–2003
> **Secretary (Receptionist),** Marketing Department
> - Screened all incoming calls and visitors.
> - Maintained knowledge of location/work status of all executives in the marketing department.
> - Controlled flow of information into/out of the department.
> - Projected a professional image for the department at all times.
> - Also provided general office support as needed.

The same secretary seeking a job as executive assistant:

Mutual Benevolent of Omaha, Omaha, Nebraska, 2001–2003
**Secretary (Assistant to the V.P. Marketing),** Marketing Department

- Provided office and administrative support to the V.P. Marketing and other executives in the marketing department.
- Prepared documents for release, including letters, memos, and product information. Drafted official correspondence for signature by the V.P. Marketing.
- Prepared complex travel itineraries for executives and marketing teams.
- Also served as front desk/receptionist for the department.

Repeat this ranking and selecting process for all information you present, going back roughly ten to fifteen years of work history. Remember to pay attention to design as you transfer this information onto your rough draft. **You are well on your way to a dynamic résumé.**

To assist you, here are a few sample experience listings. Your listings do not need to be as long as these to be effective, but do not make them so short they do not stick in the mind.

## Samples

**Amalgamated Federated Bank, NT&SA,** New York, New York
**Manager, Wholesale Receivables**                                  1998–2001

Directed billing and collections for $100,000,000 in corporate fee receivables from the bank's largest clients (all Fortune 500). Staff of six.

- Developed QA program to track productivity individually and departmentwide. Successfully reduced staff by 50 percent with concurrent increase in productivity overall.
- Recovered $243,000 in unbilled fees in internal audit; created database and new operating procedures to prevent future underbilling problems.
- Co-designed application to track LBO fees to comply with FASB regulations.

**Manager, Bank Secrecy Compliance**                                  1995–1997

Recruited by S.V.P. to design bankwide policies and procedures to achieve compliance with federal Bank Secrecy Act.

- Analyzed information and form flow bankwide. Developed and implemented policies, procedures, and training programs.
- Reduced and streamlined form flow, saving $389,000 in the first year and annually thereafter.
- Reduced error rate from 78 percent to 2 percent in six-month period.
- Developed supporting research proving improvement, resulting in 87.5 percent reduction of multimillion-dollar fine from the IRS.

**APEX, ZENITH & ACME, MANAGEMENT CONSULTANTS, Chicago, Illinois** 2000–Present
**Executive Assistant to the CEO**

Manage CEO's calendar, daily schedule, and extensive travel arrangements. Represent the CEO within the organization, to our 75 affiliated management consulting firms, and directly to clients. Control information flow into and out of the executive suite. Plan and coordinate meetings, conferences, and other events nationwide. Solve problems as they arise. Ensure CEO has all information and resources required for maximum efficiency.

- Hand-picked for this position by the CEO. Have achieved his complete respect and trust. *Excellent recommendation available.*

- Increased flow of information between CEO, officers, and the 75 affiliates. CEO increased travel commitments *and* increased day-to-day control over this diversified company.

- Facilitated development of new five-year strategic business plan, by handling related studies and research projects promptly (completed ahead of schedule).

- Developed and implemented a "real time" commitment tracking system to record, track and control the CEO's obligations moment-by-moment.

- Managed relationships with 75 affiliate firms so well that much of this responsibility was delegated to me directly.

- Due to increase in efficiency in CEO's offices, was able to eliminate one position through attrition, resulting in savings in excess of $50,000 per annum.

---

**RESTAURANT MANAGEMENT SYSTEMS, INC.**, Detroit, Michigan          2000–Present

**Unit Manager**

- Manage all aspects of high-volume corporate-owned restaurant. Full P&L responsibility, reporting to the district manager. Strong profit performance in prior units led to assignment to this major, high-volume unit. Consistently exceed objectives for gross, net, and share.

- Hire, train, motivate staff of 34. Have gained the trust and support of personnel working in a multicultural, multiracial environment. Enjoy high staff morale and lowest turnover in the district. Personally committed to production of a top-quality product in a clean, sanitary, and attractive environment.

*Selected Accomplishments:*

Achieved 17.25 percent volume increase and 15.9 percent profit increase in first assignment as unit manager. Promoted to higher volume store. Achieved 22.05 percent volume increase and 19.0 percent profit increase. Earned Top Manager Award. Earned Profit Increase Award. Earned two Volume Increase Awards. Earned two QSC Awards (quality, service, cleanliness). Earned two cash bonuses for staff recruitment. Earned two incentive trips to Hawaii. Received two courses of advanced management training. Earned Top Ten dinner with the president (top 10 percent nationwide).

---

**ArtTech Applications,** Boston, Massachusetts          1998–Present
(a subsidiary of **Mega-Size Computer Corp.**)

**President**

- Recruited by the CEO of Mega-Size to turn around negative revenue trends at this wholly owned subsidiary, a manufacturer of factory flow workstations. Hired aggressive and focused management team. Reorganized accounting and control. Reduced sales force by 20 percent; removed cap on commissions and improved incentive for outstanding performance. Stabilized cash flow by locking major customers into exclusive annualized agreements. Increased international sales by 45 percent; negotiated first joint ventures with both Japanese and German business partners.

- Identified $2 billion market for product in R&D stage, a painting process control system; accelerated release, achieving full commercialization in just eight months. Rewrote business plan with new product, regained lender confidence, renegotiated terms on $6.2 million in borrowing.

- Created and managed rapid growth, form $12 million to $87 million in less than three years, with jump in ROS from 4 percent to 16 percent. Currently seeking new challenges.

## Engineers and Consultants

There is a variation on the above style used by engineers and consultants, and that is to list projects as accomplishments. Consultants and engineers will give a scope statement covering the *type* of responsibilities they normally assume; then they will describe projects or engagements. Here are two examples:

**Holman-Johnston, Engineers**                                      Houston, Texas

**Vice President, Field Operations** and **Civil / Structural Engineer**      1998–Present

Holman-Johnston is a quality-oriented global engineering company, annual revenues of US$600,000,000, world leader in design-build of offshore structures, including traditional steel platforms and experimental designs.

Field engineering manager in charge, offshore platform installation projects. Project planning, offshore fabrication, local labor and vendor selection and oversight, client liaison. Typically in charge of approximately 50 site personnel.

*Sample projects:*

- **Field Engineer,** Jolliet TLWP floating platform for Chevron, installed in 1712 feet of water in the Gulf of Mexico. This was a first-of-its-kind installation. Supervised and coordinated 60 welders, riggers, divers, surveyors, tugboat captains, and marine crane operators. Developed classes and trained foremen, engineers, winch drivers, mates, and others every day for two weeks, before installation of never-before-tried engineering plans.

- **Company Representative,** Gulf Marine Fabricators, Aransas Pass, Texas. Verified compliance with design provided by our engineering department. Updated scheduling and field progress reports with home office. Modified rigging layout, reducing costs by 8 percent on over 1 mile of heavy installation. Supervised during jacket load out (24,000 tons).

- **Field Engineer and Construction Supervisor,** British Petroleum, North Sea. Supervised launch and pile barges for ULA platforms, in charge of 80 welders, riggers, foremen, and inspectors under extremely harsh weather conditions.

Also had office engineering management and planning assignments in between field projects (20 percent of total duty time).

**Linda C. Akizarny** dba **Marketing Design Group**, 2000–Present
Philadelphia, Pennsylvania

*Marketing Consultant*

Initiated, structured, and conducted marketing consulting projects, including all phases of business analysis, market analysis, demographic analysis, site selection, image development, and media planning.

*Sample engagements:*

- New Faces, Education Division — Provided start-up marketing plans for a cosmetic surgery cooperative based in New England. Worked directly with the founder of the cooperative to develop realistic marketing budgets and plans for various business launch scenarios. Ongoing.

- Eastern College Of Applied Technology — Revamped marketing and advertising functions for this educational nonprofit with 15 campuses. Restructured $3 million annual combined advertising/marketing budget. Solicited, reviewed, and selected an advertising agency. Consolidated and standardized planning for all campuses. Achieved 41 percent increase in applications with no increase in budget. 2001.

- Papyrus, Inc. — Retained to establish structure and internal marketing function for newly formed franchise/real estate department for an aggressive new retail chain. Provided competitive analysis, consulted on site selection, collaborated on business plan development and strategic plan for franchise development. 2000.

---

By the way, if you are tempted to list consulting to cover a period of unemployment, you will need to list actual, verifiable engagements like the ones above to achieve any credibility at all. Remember, anything you say in your résumé can and will be tested in an interview, so never make up experiences that didn't happen as they are described.

## What to Do about Common Problems

Whenever I give a lecture, somebody always asks me some version of "What do I do with unrelated jobs?" Either make them relevant or leave them out. Use the résumé "ingredients rule" and your own creativity to demonstrate how the experience would support your next job objective.

The following listing shows a restaurant worker's intelligence, sales skill, and business savvy:

**Neptune's Sea Palace,** Miami, Florida                    2000–Present
**Food Server**

Act as a "sales representative" for the restaurant, selling add-ons and extras to achieve one of the higher per-ticket and per-night sales averages. Prioritize and juggle dozens of simultaneous responsibilities. Have built loyal clientele of regulars, in addition to tourist trade. Use computer daily.

The next listing shows how a menial job at a letter-sorting machine can be used to support a candidacy for beginning systems analyst. The résumé reader may not know what an L.S.M. is, but you can be sure that he will be favorably impressed by this job listing:

**U.S.P.S. (United States Postal Service)**                                   2000–2001
**L.S.M. Operator**

> Worked average of 50–60 hours per week while full-time student, demonstrating work ethic, endurance, and sustained efficiency. Comfortable with large volume of responsibility. Excellent accuracy under deadline and in fast-paced work environment.

The prior listing illustrates a very good point about résumés: Your reader does not have to understand exactly what you have written, or exactly what you have done, as long as every possible interpretation is positive. Never be vague by accident; be vague on purpose.

Another common question is "What do I do if I have no valuable work history?" Whenever this question comes up, I think of a woman who walked into my first career consulting office, many years ago. She told me she had never had a job, she had never even worked, and while we were on the subject, she couldn't do anything anyway.

As I was interviewing her in preparation for some serious creative writing, I discovered that she had been the bookkeeper for her husband's business for ten years. Her husband ran a floating fish-processing factory in Alaska, a "seasonal business" she called it. How big? "About $3.5 million dollars, more or less, depending on the season. And I guess I do manage our rental properties while he's gone every year." What did that entail? "Well, I buy property, fix it up, and rent it out." It turned out she was in total charge of the properties, a $2 million portfolio back when that was a lot of property.

Your case will be different, but I think you get the point. **Think.** You are bound to have some valuable history. Remember to consider your part-time, temporary, avocational, or philanthropic experience.

College students can make particular use of student activities, informal experience, and classroom projects to show their skills and abilities. Here are three examples:

---

Black Student Union, Midland University                         Midland Delta, Mississippi

**President**                                                                          2000–2001

> Provided leadership to a student organization representing 22 percent of the total student body. Liaison to university administration. Member, Minority Student Affairs Board.
>
> *Selected contributions:*
>
> • Improved the image and the relevancy of the organization campuswide.
> • Increased budget by 40 percent and membership by over 100 percent.
> • Obtained changes in the university's hiring policies to promote hiring of minority faculty.
> • Organized the first-ever All South Minority Student Affairs Conference, 2001.

---

**Captain, U.C.S.B. Sailing Team**

- Planned and coordinated weekly regattas involving up to 40 competing students and an official race committee of 10.
- Obtained club sponsorship by the Santa Barbara Yacht Club, including underwriting competitive events and purchase of two new boats.

---

University of Wisconsin, Madison, 2000–2001

**Research Associate**, Chemistry Department

- Conducted experiments in strict accordance with written methodologies to originate data used in Prof. Pritchard's articles published in the *Journal of the American Chemical Society* (JACS).

For more on student résumés, see the next chapter, "Education and Additional Data."

⏤ ⏤

If you honestly lack valuable or related experience, **get some.** Volunteer, take a class, take a lower-level position to gain exposure. Demonstrate and substantiate your interest in your career objective. I had a client who had tried unsuccessfully for over two years to get into city planning. I encouraged him to sign up for some classes. He did, and we listed on his résumé that he was an *enrollee* in a city planning program. With his new résumé, demonstrating his *intention* to take some classes, he got a job in city planning before the first class even started. To his credit, he continued the program and eventually got his master's degree.

⏤ ⏤

What do you do if you are self-employed? Employers have justified fears of the self-employed. The two main fears are that you are too independent to take orders and fit into an organizational structure and that you will learn their business and go into competition against them. Pretty scary fears, right? Do yourself a favor. Downplay self-employment as much as possible. Decide if you can call yourself "manager" instead of "president." Do not call the company "Albert Bernard Chasworth, Inc.," call it "ABC, Inc." There are exceptions, of course, but a word to the wise is sufficient. Once you are in the interview, reveal all. This type of technique is valid to get into an interview, but it is a mistake to carry it too far.

⏤ ⏤

What do you do with military experience? If it is recent, treat it *exactly* like any other kind of experience. **Remove the military jargon** and stress the interpersonal, leadership, and organizational aspects of your experience. Say *workers* not *soldiers* and *equipment* not *tanks* or *weapons.* You'll get extra points if you can work in common business terms like *profit, ROI,* and *sales.*

If your military service is ancient history, you may omit it or give it a quick listing with a heading of its own, like this:

**MILITARY**

**Colonel (ret.), United States Marine Corps**

Navy Cross (second highest U. S. military award for heroism in combat)

Bronze Star (2), Purple Heart (2)

If you are proud of your service or it demonstrates important job skills, then list it. If you think it is irrelevant to your current career, leave it out.

What do you do if your most important jobs fall behind unimportant or unimpressive jobs? The answer is simple: reorder them or regroup them. As mentioned earlier, you can regroup your jobs under subheadings, such as "Related Experience" and "Additional Experience," or "Management Experience" and "Sales Experience," but you can also just reorder your jobs altogether. Consider listing your jobs out of chronological order. Put them **in order of interest to your targeted reader.** Keep the dates accurate, or remove them altogether (see below).

### Gaps, Dates, and More Problems

What do you do about job gaps? This is really a date question. There are many good reasons for job gaps, and it is perfectly acceptable to have a gap somewhere in your career as long as you can explain it in an interview. My suggestion is simple: Show the gap without comment and be prepared to discuss it in an interview or telephone inquiry from the hiring authority.

**"This is the best I can do for 'previous employment.'"**

Do not fill in the missing time on your résumé with some excusatory line like, "1996–1999, family obligations." Such a line does not support your candidacy in any way. Be sure you do not fall for the temptation to "adjust" dates from legitimate experience to cover gaps. Fudging on your dates is very dangerous, and the risk is simply not proportional to the gain. See Résumé Writing Rule #4, page 6.

There are several ways to obscure and deemphasize dates, the chief of which is to list dates by year only. The real point is that modern employers are not fixated on continuous employment. *Most* workers have gaps in their employment now. I am in favor of deemphasizing dates on general principle. Dates do not of themselves demonstrate a job skill or talent.

What if you have not worked in over a year? This is another date question. One of my favorite techniques for this is to take a reading like "1996–1999" and let it read open-ended, "1996–," as though you meant "1996–Present." This is called the tombstone technique. In résumés, curiosity will almost always work in your favor. Here is how it might look:

> **Jorgensen & Daughters General Contractors,** 1996–
> **Project Manager**

Another date technique is to list experience as "current" and "prior" without specifying any dates at all. Avoid using duration, such as "two years" or "six years," where you would have put the actual dates. This is distracting and raises far more questions than it answers.

It is okay to leave dates out entirely, but you will face some suspicion if you do. This suspicion, however, is often an easier liability to overcome than the liability revealed by the dates themselves. Some of the résumé samples in chapters 11 and 12 have omitted or purposely obfuscated the dates, all without telling a lie. See the résumé for Barbara Hermann on page 91, for Dean Rodgers on page 65, and Wade A. Stevenson on page 66.

What do you do about too many jobs, too many cities, and so on? It should be obvious by now: If you have too many jobs, omit some. If every job is in a new city, omit all the cities. Look at the following two chronologies, the same work history presented in two very different ways:

| | |
|---|---|
| **Truck Driver,** XYZ Industrial Plant, Louisville, Kentucky | 9/2000–Present |
| **Fire Fighter,** U.S. Bureau of Lumber & Mines, Wenatchee, Washington | 6/2000–9/2000 |
| **Delivery Driver,** Sno-Frost Cake & Candy, Dallas, Texas | 12/1999–1/2000 |
| **Welder's Assistant,** Firefly Offshore Oil Field Supply, Grand Isle, Louisiana | 6/1999–8/1999 |
| **Forklift Driver,** Empire Building Supply, Ithaca, New York | 6/1998–3/1999 |
| **Bartender,** Hemingway's, Key West, Florida | 4/1998–6/1998 |
| **Tow Truck Driver,** Able Towing & Road Service, Winnemucca, Nevada | 12/1996–1/1998 |

What do you think of this candidate? Unreliable, a "road scholar." Now look what happens if you take an eraser to this background:

| | |
|---|---|
| **Truck Driver,** XYZ Industrial Plant | 2000–Present |
| **Delivery Driver,** Sno-Frost Cake & Candy | 1999–2000 |
| **Forklift Driver,** Empire Building Supply | 1998–1999 |
| **Tow Truck Driver,** Able Towing & Road Service | 1996–1998 |

This is still quite a few jobs, but I see a definite career path and, for a driver, reasonable duration. Tell me this candidate has a clean driving record, no tickets, and no accidents in the last seven years, and I may be interested.

Sometimes the best thing you can do with some of your information is *leave it out.*

The special challenges of scannable résumés and electronic résumé styles are covered in chapter 13, "Scannable, Internet, and HTML Electronic Résumés," beginning on page 95.

Hopefully by now you are getting a feel for the approach to solving these problems. Do not learn a handful of tricks from this book. Learn a way of thinking. Then you can solve your own problem, no matter how unusual it may be.

# Writing Your Résumé: Education and Additional Data

## CHAPTER 10

If your career has progressed logically and is well represented by your experience, your education can be rather briefly stated, with or without dates.

**M.B.A.,** Howard University, Washington, D.C.

**B.S.,** Economics, Duke University, Durham, North Carolina

The following education listings cover most typical cases. Some are a little more creative than others, but all are common and accepted practice.

**B.S.B.A.** (Bachelor of Science in Business Administration), *ongoing*
Arizona State University, Tempe

---

**M.D., Harvard Medical School,** Boston, Massachusetts, 1998
**B.A., Biology, Reed College,** Portland, Oregon, 1994

---

**B.A., Marketing,** S.U.N.Y., Buffalo, expected 2003

---

**M.S.S.W.** (Master of Science Program in Social Work), *enrollee*
University of Texas, Arlington

---

**B.A.** (Bachelor of Arts in Psychology), 1999
University of Texas, Dallas

---

**Ph.D.** (ABD), Anthropology, 2000
**B.S.,** Anthropology, *magna cum laude*, 1996
University of California, Berkeley

*ABD* stands for "all but dissertation." Similarly, *ABT* stands for "all but thesis." These are two of the handiest little abbreviations in higher education today.

If you abandoned an advanced degree program, do not write "M.B.A. Candidate, 1992–1993." Instead, turn it into a positive statement, as in the following:

**Graduate Studies in Finance and Business Analysis,** 1992–1993

Golden Gate University, San Francisco

If you have a B.A. in music history and you are now an accountant, you may wish to list your undergraduate degree without specifying a major.

**B.A., Boston University,** Boston, Massachusetts

If you went to school but did not graduate, do not claim a degree. Anybody can call any registrar's office in America, say, "I'm calling to verify a degree," and less than sixty seconds later they will know the truth of the matter. (Incidentally, if you hire people, make it a point to check.) If you took even one college course, you can use a listing like the following:

**Psychology,** Tulane University, New Orleans, Louisiana

It won't work in all cases, but if you have experience and manage your job search well, you will definitely receive consideration and you will get a good job. Accept your shortcomings *whatever they may be.* Your education will only be a stumbling block if you let it be one.

If your education is truly nonexistent, then omit it. I have had only one professional candidate in my executive coaching career who did not have any college education at all—not one day in a college classroom, not one management seminar, nothing. He had dropped out of high school to become a super-roadie, designing one-of-a-kind audio equipment and high-tech visual effects for alternative rock bands, and after several career twists, he had become a process automation engineer.

So we left education off entirely. He had a very impressive two-page résumé, which was handy because whichever page the reader was on, he could assume the education was on the other. It worked. My client was flown across the continent for interviews with an exciting robotics engineering firm. They even negotiated an offer before the matter finally came up. When it did come up, my candidate was ready: "All my life I have been working on cutting-edge technology, and frankly, I just couldn't take the time out to go to school to study science that was obsolete."

He got the job.

Whatever your limitations may be, accept them and go on. Get out there and sell yourself on your strengths.

After you have a good job, then really think about getting that degree. No matter how old you are, you will not get any younger, and to paraphrase Dear Abby, how old will you be in X years if you *don't* get that degree now? Also, as people change jobs more frequently, it is a nuisance to have to run this gauntlet over and over again.

Even if you have one degree, if you are under thirty-five, you had better seriously think about an advanced degree. Your case may be an exception, but I am seeing more and more careers choked off because of the lack of an M.B.A. or other advanced education. This is particularly true in the fast lane of business, but also in any lane of education, social services, science, engineering, and even such unlikely fields as the military. Not everyone wants more and more career challenges, but if you do, take a hard look at your credentials.

Recent college graduates can make a big presentation out of their education section. It can include classes, honors, awards, activities, affiliations, study abroad, special projects, their golf handicap, and practically anything you can imagine. If recent education is one of your greatest qualifications for a position, feel free to feature items like these:

**University of Nevada,** Las Vegas, Nevada

Candidate for the **Bachelor of Science in Hotel Administration** expected May 2002

> Dean's Honors
>
> St. Tropez Partnership Scholarship
>
> Hotel Association
>
> Eta Sigma Delta, International Hospitality Management Honor Society Vice President
>
> Professional Convention Management Association
>
> Champion, Intramural Squash

One thing that you should be careful in presenting, however, is affiliation with a non-academic sorority or fraternity. If you were president, vice president, or treasurer, feature your leadership experience and contributions. Admitting that you chaired the social committee, on the other hand, is tantamount to admitting that you are an expert at drinking beer. In fact, not only are you an expert at this arcane skill, but you teach this skill to others. Show a little wisdom and talk about your community service projects.

The most compelling college-related listings will be actual classes taken. Use the word *coursework* so you can paraphrase class titles somewhat more freely.

**B.S., Business Administration,** 2001

Michigan State University

*Coursework included:*

- Accounting I and II
- Corporate Finance
- Statistics I & II
- Sales & Sales Management
- Marketing Strategy & Planning
- Marketing Research

*Computer skills:*

- HTML Programming & Web Page Design
- Spreadsheet Applications
- Java
- Database Applications

This technique is particularly useful for featuring classes you may have taken outside your major, if they support your career objective.

If education is one of your only qualifications for your next position, you may also choose to pull out special projects and make them listings unto themselves. Just use a heading like **"SPECIAL PROJECTS"** and go on to write them up like experience listings (see the previous chapter). People who have programmed applications, solved marketing problems, designed and specified the interior of a four-hundred-seat restaurant (as school projects) will be able to get a lot of mileage out of this technique.

Finally, if you have no college experience and want to list a high school diploma, even that can be spiced up:

**Diploma, College Preparatory Studies,** 1998

Central High School, Middletown, Ohio

- High scores in math and science.
- "Athletic Scholar" award for simultaneous letter and honor roll.

In the Northeast, it is common to list prep schools on résumés, particularly in certain industries, such as finance. West of the Atlantic Seaboard, I would probably recommend against it. In much of the United States, Phillips Exeter might sound more like a tobacco product than an elite academy.

Finally, if your education is overwhelming or irrelevant, leave some out or put it at the bottom of your résumé in a section on "Additional Education." I actually saw a candidate from Florida with this listing at the bottom of his résumé: HOBBIES: Ph.D., Astrophysics.

Write your education section *now*.

Then as you proceed through the following sections, add in pertinent data or additional headings as needed.

## Professional Credentials and Licenses

Professional credentials can be cited either at the top of the résumé or with the education. Do not assume that your reader will realize you have professional credentials because of your experience.

**C.P.A.,** State of California, since 1982

**Member,** State Bar of New York, admitted 1995

**NASD Series 7 License,** current

Credentials can also be listed as "pending," if you are writing your résumé after you have sat for the exam, and before the results are released.

## Languages

The business world is increasingly international. If you are even remotely likely to use a language skill in your next job, list it either in your profile or under your education or in a heading by itself or somewhere under an **"Additional"** heading at the bottom of your résumé (see below). Remember, the more important the skill is the more likely it belongs in your profile. For the sixth time: **Put the information in order of interest to your targeted reader.**

## Affiliations, Community Service, Activities

As a general rule, these categories strengthen a weak candidate and weaken a strong candidate. In any case, only the most *directly related* and *candidacy-supporting* organizations should be listed.

For example, if you are interested in a position in import/export, belonging to the World Trade Club might be seen as a plus. If you are an import/export executive, unless you are an officer of the organization or a featured speaker, you might forgo the listing.

Be sure to skip organizations whose chief criterion for membership is the ability to write a check. Everybody in hiring knows which organizations those are.

Another use for this section is to reveal your ethnic identity. If you wish to reveal that you are gay, or African American, or Azerbaijani, here is one place to do it. There is no doubt that membership in the Azerbaijani Students Association identifies you as Azerbaijani.

I used to think that such identifications had no place on a résumé, ever, but my point of view is changing. I tried to take an organization off a gentleman's résumé because it identified him as gay. He was very clear about why he wanted it put back: "I don't care to work in an office that is homophobic."

Although I can understand this sentiment, it is still my professional opinion that any information that can play to an employer's base prejudices, for *or* against the candidate, should be avoided. Your ability to perform your duties should be the focus of your résumé, not your status as a former model, minority, or member of a particular church.

Get the interview based on your job skills, as clearly presented on your résumé. Then use your professionalism, personality, and the strength of your qualifications to overcome any unfair and irrelevant prejudices your employer may have. If you do a good job of answering the question "What can this candidate do for me?" your potential employer is not going to care if you are a green Martian.

In addition to avoiding unnecessary ethnic identifications, be careful of using this section to make a statement about your personality, politics, or lifestyle.

Yoga may be a life-enriching activity for you, but mentioning it may make you seem flaky to your potential employer. Your status as a deacon in a Baptist church may be a negative factor to someone who is Jewish or Roman Catholic. Even your sports activities may be an unconscious turnoff to the tired, cigarette-smoking vice president who reads your résumé at 9 P.M.

These types of information have their own name in résumé jargon: *throw-out factors.* They are either irrelevant or personal data that do little or nothing to advance your candidacy, yet create a great potential for your résumé to be thrown out. In business terms, the possible upside is small, the possible downside is terminal.

If you really plan to entertain clients on the links, then maybe you should mention your golf talents. However, the general rule is that, unless you plan to do it on your job, leave it out.

### Hobbies

For 99.44 percent of people reading this sentence, listing hobbies on your résumé will be fluff. Once again, only the most *directly related* and *candidacy-supporting* hobbies should be listed.

In all my years of writing résumés, I can only think of one instance that exemplifies a directly related and candidacy-supporting hobby. This particular client was an electronics technician whose hobby was designing robots for amusement. Apparently, he was a real Rube Goldberg, with a house full of robots to fetch coffee, vacuum the floor, chase the kids, you name it. If your hobby is not this strongly related to your objective, I would leave it out.

### Additional

You can put a grab bag heading such as this near the bottom of your résumé. This section can contain foreign-language skills, relevant travel experiences, availability, and any loose items that you feel are important to convey to a potential employer. I try to avoid needing to write a section like this, but it is common enough to have one.

There is a résumé-writing theory that says you should end your résumé with one last punch, but I do not agree with it. Your résumé should have its punch at the top and wind down toward the end. I certainly would not wait until this section to introduce critical information. If your qualifications are less than perfect, however, you may wish to throw a few final hooks in the end, to try to stay in the "yes" pile.

### *Examples*

> Proven performer with a desire to tackle a new challenge. Comfortable with high-end, sophisticated, and/or technical products. Available for unlimited travel as needed.

---

> Aspiring writer with the talent and the desire to succeed on both professional and personal levels in extremely competitive environments. Self-directed, highly energetic. Completed bachelor of arts degree while working full time. Contagious intellectual curiosity and enthusiasm. Committed to the pursuit of excellence in work and lifelong learning.

---

### Personal Section

If you are not a native citizen or are likely to be identified as such, I recommend that you identify your status: Under a "**PERSONAL**" section, state that you are a "Resident alien, valid 'green card,' qualified for immediate employment," "U.S. citizen since 1995," or "Canadian citizen since 1973."

In an American business résumé, you should *never* list your height, weight, physical condition, age or date of birth, marital status, names of your kids, social security number, or similar personal data. You immediately identify yourself as a "résumé dinosaur" who has not read a résumé book since 1958. This is not funny. Your potential employer will assume that all of your management ideas are from 1958, too.

On the other hand, if you are applying for work internationally, you should know that the entire rest of the world lists date of birth and marital status, at least. (In Japan, employers want to know which grammar school you attended, so they can discern the neighborhood you grew up in, and presumably what kind of person you are.) If you send your résumé overseas, include basic personal data, but not height and weight. The following listing was designed to allow the client to use his résumé anywhere in the world:

**PERSONAL:**

Available for travel and offshore assignments for the right company.

Date of Birth: February 2, 1970.

Citizenship: United Kingdom. Passport: United Kingdom.

Married to U.S. Citizen. Status: U.S. Resident Alien, valid "Green Card."

Qualified to work throughout the U.S. and Europe, without reservations.

References and additional details provided on interview.

## References

Do not list your references on your résumé, no matter who they are. References, portfolio, transcripts, writing samples, lists of publications, and the like can all be offered on request.

Some people end their résumés with a cautionary note: "References gladly provided upon request, but please keep this application confidential at this time." This might be particularly pertinent if your current employer is happy with your work and doesn't know you are looking for a new job. Of course, that's not a bad image to leave a prospective employer with, either: that is, that you're valued where you are now.

As a general rule, you can forego the rote statement "References on request." It is considered understood, and therefore a waste of words. If you're not going to put some twist on the line, it's best just to leave it out.

Think over your whole background. Is there some skill or credential that is tangential enough to be distracting in your profile, but important enough to include near the bottom of your presentation? If so, add it in *now*.

**Congratulations. The first draft of your résumé is done.**

# *Writing Your Résumé: Putting It Together*

## CHAPTER 11

Take a long look at the first draft of your résumé. How does it look? How do you feel?

Most of us find the act of putting together a résumé exhilarating, even cathartic. Seldom in life do we sit back and really take account of our accomplishments. In a thousand ways, every one of us is an unsung hero. This is one chance we have to sing that song. Take a moment to savor it.

Now look again. Think. Did you leave anything out? If you did, stop now and put it in. Do not worry about how long your résumé is. We will address that in a moment. When you are satisfied that everything that needs to be in your résumé is in it, only then will we proceed to take things out.

## Final Edit

There are several techniques to shorten, strengthen, and improve your presentation. To put it simply: Throw things out or summarize them.

Ernest Hemingway called his eraser a "shit detector." Take a look at your sentences. How many adjectives can be thrown out? How many statements will be obvious to your intended reader? Check your résumé for tone. Be especially wary of sounding pompous. *Excellent* and *outstanding*, when applied to yourself, can have an unintended effect on the reader.

Your résumé should wind down toward the end. As a general rule, each job listing should be a little shorter than the last. Give your recent experience full exposure, but as you get back to ten or fifteen years ago, just stop. This has a very interesting effect. If you remove dates from your education, it is impossible to date you. You cannot be discriminated against because of your age, whatever it is, since your age is not available.

Employers have a profile in mind of the candidate they are looking for. That profile can be very specific. This is not really a form of prejudice—though it can work out that way— just standard management planning. The best managers think visually, they project the future visually, and you may not be in that vision. So revealing data that can be counted against you, *even subconsciously,* is something you should avoid. Once you are in the interview, you can easily demonstrate why you are the right person for the job, even if you were not the candidate they had in mind. Do not let subconscious prejudices keep you from getting an interview. Keep throw-out factors out of your résumé.

Besides, few banking vice presidents are stronger candidates because of a full delineation of their duties as a "Vault Teller" early in their career. If you have older experience that you feel supports your candidacy, use an encompassing statement without dates:

**PRIOR:**

**Executive Assistant to the CEO,** Ajax & MacDonald Machine Tool Co., Akron, Ohio

**Office Manager,** Dewey, Cheatham & Howe, New York, New York

The same technique works under education:

**ADDITIONAL:**

**Technical Training, Workshops & Seminars** (numerous)

Now look your résumé over and see if anything is annoying to you. If it is, it is probably not true, or not you. If it is not true, take it out. If it is not you, but it is true and it will improve your candidacy, *try to leave it in.* This is no time to be humble.

The acid test for whether your résumé is true is this: Would you be comfortable sharing this résumé with your references? If so, go for it. If not, it is probably misleading or overstated in a way that will get you in trouble later anyway. Work it over until it is background check–proof.

I know from experience that some people are not comfortable with profiles that state their skills and abilities. If everything in your profile is true, factual, and not pompous, then go with it. If you are using your résumé inside your own company, or applying to a position through a direct, guaranteed contact, then you might decide to drop your profile. (If you do drop your profile, save the wording. Often it can be included in your cover letter, sometimes verbatim.) Without the profile, your résumé will be better because you wrote a profile first, and it helped focus your thoughts throughout. If you are going to face heavy, direct competition—or if you are applying to people who are in no way obligated to speak with you—then I would recommend you use the best profile you can write.

Finally, check your résumé for point of view one last time. Is everything really in the order of maximum desired impact on the reader? Take your time with this. The order of your information is second in importance only to the information itself. Think about your reader. **Put your information in order of interest to the targeted reader.**

Except for the grammar and spelling, do not be a perfectionist. A perfectionist will still be working on his résumé long after you have a great new job.

## Production

Unless you have a computer and printer at your disposal, you will need to contract for word processing and printing. Look in the Yellow Pages under copy centers, to see if they provide computer rental by the minute, or call secretarial or word processing services or résumé services. If you need any final design assistance or want to have a second opinion on your résumé, consider an exploratory meeting with a résumé service, but remember, in the end it's your résumé and you're the one who will be going to interviews and explaining what's on your résumé.

Don't be surprised if you have to tinker with your résumé to get the design just right. Fonts and type sizes are different on different systems. You will need to verify that you like the spacing, layout, and overall design in its final form.

If you are a management-level candidate, I recommend a conservative presentation. A very simple border, at most, might be okay, but otherwise avoid fancy layouts and designs, details such as little pointing hands, and other bells and whistles. These detract from your qualifications.

Whatever you do, do not let someone talk you into some kind of foldout or brochure format. These are ostentatious and notoriously unpopular with employers. Use standard-size paper. Use white or very light grey paper if you are an executive. Others can use off-white paper of various hues, but I would think more than twice about pink or blue. White is really the best choice, as it can be copied, scanned, or faxed without loss of readability.

The weight of the paper is actually as important as the color. I recommend heavy paper, as it subconsciously denotes a candidate with substance. If you hand someone a stack of résumés, she will pick a disproportionate percentage of ones on heavy paper.

Once you are happy with your design, either print it straight from the computer on a laser printer, or photocopy it from a master on a commercial-grade photocopying machine. The quality of these copying machines is so high now that only a graphic artist would notice the difference between the copy and the original. Better papers will usually have a watermark, so no matter how you print the final version, be sure that the watermark on the paper is right-side up. Printing onto the paper upside down or backwards is indicative of a sloppy, inattentive candidate.

While you are printing your résumé, get some nine-by-twelve envelopes. Your beautiful résumé should not arrive all folded up, with the print flaking off. It should arrive flat, like any quality presentation. I prefer white nine-by-twelve envelopes, which are known as *catalog envelopes.* Do not forget, a nine-by-twelve envelope requires extra postage, even if it is under one ounce. It would not be graceful for your résumé to arrive with postage due.

Your overnight résumé is now done. If you are not mailing your résumé and do not need a cover letter, you can skip the rest of this book. You might want to read the section entitled "Job Search Protocol" in the next chapter, however, as it applies to practically everybody. *Good luck!*

## Additional Assistance

The following pages contain complete samples of well-designed résumés. Look them over as a guide, but do not copy any sentences verbatim. Résumé styles change and evolve, and today's hot phrase is tomorrow's cliché. (For instance, it's the opposite of progressive to use the word *progressive*). The best way to make sure your résumé is fresh is by writing it yourself.

If you decide you need additional help, there are two good sources: your friends and a résumé-writing professional.

Do not be worried or surprised if you get ten different opinions when you show your résumé to six different friends. Use the principles outlined in this book and your own good judgment to sort through their suggestions for the ones you think are valid.

If you use a résumé-writing professional, be sure to shop around. Ask to see samples, make sure the design is good, and make sure the person you're meeting with actually wrote them. Then be sure to read them. A good design is worthless if there are typos and errors in the work. Finally, your writer should have a good, honest approach. Hype and fluff are damaging to a well-qualified candidate.

For more on **scannable** and **Internet résumés,** be sure to see chapter 13, "Scannable, Internet, and HTML Electronic Résumés."

# JOSEPHINE JUDDLEY

199 Minna Street
San Francisco, California 94105

Telephone/message: (415) 555-7730
JJ@pac.net

**INTERESTS**    **Financial Analysis / Investment Analysis**

High technical/analytical aptitude. Demonstrated skill for quantitative analysis in both scientific and business applications. Special knowledge of health-care and biotech industry sectors.

Advanced user of spreadsheet programs. Advanced Web-based research skills.

Proven communication skills as demonstrated in teaching and leadership roles in extracurricular and employment settings.

Conversational Spanish.

**EDUCATION**    UNIVERSITY OF CALIFORNIA, Santa Barbara, California

*degrees*    **B.A., Accounting,** minor in **Economics,** 2000
**B.A., Chemistry**, 2000

*activities*    Captain, UCSB Sailing Team
Captain, USC Sailing Team (USC, 1997–1998)
- Planned and coordinated weekly regattas involving up to 40 competing students and an official race committee of 10.

*project*   
- Conducted short- and long-range investment analyses on NYSE stocks using WebTicker. Tested company valuation principles in relation to actual stock values. Tested market trend theories.
- Studied LBOs of eight companies from origination in the 1980s. Developed methodologies to forecast LBO success or failure based on regression analysis.
- Completed a business valuation study on a $270 million subsidiary of a Fortune 100 company as part of a potential offering memorandum.

**EMPLOYMENT**    UCSB CHEMISTRY DEPARTMENT, Santa Barbara, California
**Research Associate,** 1996–1997, 1999

- Conducted experiments in strict accordance with written methodologies to originate data used in Prof. Pritchard's articles published in the *Journal of the American Chemical Society* (JACS).

SAN DIEGO YACHT CLUB, San Diego, California
**Lead Instructor,** Summer 1997

- Organized and managed summer Junior Sailing Program serving 180 students, aged 8 to 18. Trained and supervised 10 instructors. Reported to the SDYC board of directors.

PACIFIC COAST INTERCOLLEGIATE YACHT RACING ASSOCIATION, Irvine, California
**Vice President,** 1998

- Served on the board of directors. As a team, the board sets collegiate regattas for the West Coast. Our goal during this time was to strengthen and centralize the association, which we did.

# Leslie Moskowitz

23 Pinehurst Circle
Denver, Colorado 80235

Telephone/Message
(303) 555-2286

| | |
|---|---|
| **EXPERTISE** | • **Systems Administration** |
| | • **Database Management** |
| | • **IS Generalist** |

*Skillset:*
• **Communications, word processing, database,** and **spreadsheet applications,** including but not limited to: Novell LAN administration, DataEase PC-based RDBMS, Windows, e-mail systems, WordPerfect, MS Word, and many others. HW: HP and IBM, data-telecom HW, all peripherals. Available 24/7 on call.

**EXPERIENCE**

FRANCHISE RESTAURANTS, INC.                                  HQ: Denver, CO
**Systems Administrator**                                          1998–2000

Hands-on systems administrator, managing wide range of daily applications and special projects on behalf of the IS manager and others throughout the company. Supervised clerical and entry staff. Coordinated with data users company-wide.

Provided administration, security, troubleshooting, and daily backup for accounting server, fax server, databases, e-mail system, and all office automation applications. Documented systems and applications as needed.

Also ordered and managed supplies, sourced and evaluated new products, set up and integrated new systems, upgrades, and enhancements, and contributed to IS manager's planning concerning technology evolution for the company.

*Sample contributions:*
• Created a key company database, Franchise Data Information QSC Program, including database design, set-up, programming of download application (remote survey centers modem direct into database), testing/debugging/data integrity, and staff training on DB maintenance.
• Project leader for computing projects, for example, provided resources planning (time and materials), task outline, and timeline for company-wide Windows upgrades.
• Training person for other staff on DB, fax server, and Higgins e-mail systems.

**Technical Assistant, IS**                                          1995–1998
Began compiling franchise database that later became the above project. Handled route tape backups/rotations and weekly check printing. Troubleshooter for HW, SW, LAN. Designed some IS departmental procedures. Designed data presentation for a convention. Created database forms as needed.

**Data Processing Assistant, MIS**                                 1992–1994
Hired to review ten years of historical information in database and assist IS managers with design of better information extraction. Handled wide variety of routine IS functions, including data entry.

**EDUCATION &
TRAINING**

**Computer & Information Studies,** Ausbrooks Computer College, Cold Springs, CO. *Extensive* vendor training (**Novell, DataEase,** etc.). Self-taught on Internet; able to self-teach on most applications; "train self today, train others tomorrow."

# Phoebe McCoyne

12 Martinique Court, No. 2F
New York, New York 10014

Office/voicemail: (212) 555-1398
Residence/message: (212) 555-9356

## INTERESTS

**Store Management • Sales Management • New Business Development**
*Highlights:*
- One of the top 25 sales associates nationwide (out of several thousand).
- Trained in consultative and suggestive selling.
- Consistently excel at developing sales skills in subordinates.
- Proven manager and supervisor; wide range of related skills including Mac and IBM PCs (word processing, database applications, accounting), business analysis, business writing; no restrictions on business travel; available for relocation for continued advancement.
- Seeking long-term opportunity with rewards commensurate with contributions.

*Also:* Strong analytical skills. Proven affinity for high-end clientele; able to bond with customers and establish trusting relationships. Enduring contribution to the bottom line and quality of service for every employer. Organized, conscientious, responsible. Enthusiastic attitude.

## EXPERIENCE

**BEANSTALKS,** HQ: Los Angeles, CA                                    1999–Present
**Store Manager,** Manhattan
Brought on board as opening manager for the new Manhattan store, a concept store designed to test merchandising ideas for the entire Beanstalks chain. Trained in Beverly Hills and San Francisco prior to opening in Manhattan. Supervise 20 stock and sales associates, providing sales training, operational expertise, and informal motivational coaching to all staff. Analyze sales, margins, trends. Coordinate with corporate buyers in Los Angeles.
- Participated in final stages of store design. Represented Beanstalks to the contractor.
- Wrote merchandising and advertising plans for opening. Hired original staff.
- Exceeded original sales plan by 29 percent through sales training and coaching.

**NORDSTROM,** HQ: Seattle, WA                                    1997–1999
**Section Sales Manager** and **Sales Associate,** Beverly Hills, San Francisco
Top performer with the most successful major retailer in the nation. Selected to sales manage Brass Cherry, the top volume department at Nordstrom San Francisco Centre, one of the showcase stores in the chain. Sold, coached others in sales, analyzed sales, margins, and trends, reported to management. Excelled at creating a private book clientele.
- One of the top 25 sales associates nationwide.
- Top sales performer on the floor with concurrent management duties.
- "Department All Star" and "Sales Pacesetter" awards.

**AMERICAN CONGRESS ON FITNESS,** HQ: Washington, DC                                    1995–1996
**Outreach Representative (Sales)**
Developed lines of communication with national and international accounts, selling educational items and licensed exercise apparel. Practiced suggestive selling. Prepared and processed all purchase orders, including international orders. Troubleshot orders, including "walking" them through the system when needed.
- Represented American Congress on Fitness at national convention in Chicago, 1996.

**GOOD SHEPHERD HOSPITAL,** HQ: Milwaukee, WI                                    Summer 1994
**Intern, Public Relations**

## EDUCATION

**B.A., Speech Communications,** *summa cum laude,* Marquette University, Milwaukee, WI                    1995

# Pi Qi Ling

Private Line (message/fax/pager): (203) 555-6398
Office: (203) 555-2783
E-mail: pling@ucon.com

15 Noble Road
Stamford, Connecticut 06904

## STRENGTHS

**Human Resources—Generalist / Consultant / Special Projects Manager**

Senior human resources generalist with strong international business orientation and experience in recruiting, staffing, TQM, communications, HRIS, benefits, organizational development and profit and loss. Successful hands-on management experience with international and domestic staffs. Developed and managed HR functions. Key participant in business and strategic decision making. Multidisciplinary experience: human resources, operations, financials. Native fluency in English and Mandarin Chinese; conversationally fluent in French, Japanese, and several Chinese dialects.

## EDUCATION

**M.B.A.,** The Wharton School, University of Pennsylvania, Philadelphia, Pennsylvania

**B.A.,** Mathematics-Economics (double major), Reed College, Portland, Oregon

## EXPERIENCE

**WHALEN-MASTERS INTERNATIONAL,** Stamford, Connecticut

**International Human Resources Consultant,** 1999–Present

Engaged by director of international human resources to provide full-scope generalist support to 10 international joint ventures in start-up to fully-operational status, $48 million total seed monies, 32 interlocked business partners, initial staffing targets of 600+.

- Improved customer service to clients by developing "single point of contact" structure.
- Established recruiting and staffing processes, identified new sources for technical contractors, and designed and implemented new tracking and reporting methods.
- Redesigned international programs by benchmarking best practices, evaluating vendors, and identifying productivity enhancements.
- Structured short- and long-term employment packages for international assignees.

**MORROW TECHNOLABS, INC.,** Boston, Massachusetts

**Human Resources Consultant,** Taiwan, 1998

As the only human resources expert on a technical team of 36, designed and installed a DB2 Human Resources System for a national company with 12 regional offices and 40,000 employee records.

- Developed business statement and detailed conversion plan; assisted client in designing HR programs.
- Extensive formal and informal knowledge transfer/training to client and United Nations consultants involved with project.

**MIEJING USA,** Los Angeles, California

(formerly The Harmony Companies, see below)

**VP & Merger Team Member, Human Resources,** M-USA HQ, 1997

Consulted closely with country managers to resolve issues related to merger of Asian operations with a US-based acquisition, The Harmony Companies, comprised of 24 US and offshore facilities and 4300 affected staff in 12 countries. This was a fast-paced project, with heavy load of daily communications as project parameters, specifications, and objectives evolved.

- Created process framework for post-merger staff selection and successfully represented the process to country managers. Managed process; provided counsel regarding contracts and staffing issues.
- Project managed the integration of key human resource–related activities by country to ensure resolution of critical issues by merger date.
- Developed reporting method for senior management to determine country-specific human resource support, staffing, and expense levels pre- and post-merger.
- Highest-ranking officer of The Harmony Companies offered a permanent position after reorganization.

*continued . . .*

**THE HARMONY COMPANIES,** Los Angeles, California
**VP of Human Resources,** 1993–1996

Administered centralized human resource function for 4300 employees, 600 retirees, and 150 inactives, including international assignees. Managed staff of 16, planned and administered $2.8 million annual HR budget (aggregate), controlled $950,000 in US-based assets.

- Developed and successfully implemented TQM practices which proved value added to top management; built credibility for human resources by linking HR strategies to business strategies and financial measurements.
- Managed proposed and actualized M & A integration involving businesses from 100 to 2,000 employees.
- Project managed the introduction of flexible benefits corporate-wide in 10 months and within budget.
- Merged four departments, decreased staff by 23 percent, decreased total operating expenses by 17 percent.
- Served on Human Resources Information System (HRIS) Steering Committee.

**CHEMEX BANK NT & SA,** New York, New York
**VP & Manager, Training, Asia Division, Human Resources,** Regional HQ, Tokyo, Japan/Training HQ, Singapore, 1989–1993

Provided strategic direction and interpreted policy in human resources development relative to country-specific business plans, budgets and organizational development issues. In Singapore, supervised a core staff of 10 with diverse responsibility for instructional design, training, IS, and administration. Functionally responsible for development of training/personnel officers in all 15 division countries.

- Created new revenue stream of more than $1 million over four-year period by designing, negotiating contracts, and delivering fee-based training services to Korean correspondent banks, financial institutions, and government entities though Singapore center.
- Migrated corporate programs to 15 countries in the division as part of fundamental change in culture/strategy.
- Implemented corporate-wide performance planning, coaching and evaluation process in Asia Division as part of move to standardize world practices.
- Engineered downsizing of eight full-time employees and trained local continuation successor, upon completion of change project.
- Managed design, development, and piloting of standardized global Credit Training Program.

**Management Development Instructor, Corporate Human Resources**
**AVP & Head of Credit, Consumer Credit Card Center**
**Training Officer, Chemex New York**

**CONTINUING EDUCATION/PROFESSIONAL AFFILIATIONS**

American Compensation Association Certification, *in progress*
Senior Professional in Human Resources (SPHR), Human Resource Certification Institute
Society for Human Resource Management
Institute for International Human Resources

**AWARDS**

Executive Incentive Plan Award, Restricted Stock Awards, Exceptional Performance Awards

# Sheryl Yen

270 Holokai Place
Honolulu, HI 96825
(606) 555-6210
2yen@island.com

## PROFILE

Skilled small business manager with technical skills in framing and art preservation, demonstrated talent for sales and customer service, and ability to hire and supervise an intelligent and motivated staff. Experience with major commercial accounts. Back-office skills include administration, personnel management, and accounting/bookkeeping.

## SKILLS

- Mats, Specialty Cuts, Oval & Circle, Multiple Opening, Filets, Fabric Wraps
- Dry Mount, Spray Mount, Wet Mount
- Glass, Mirror, Plexi, Plexi Boxes
- Cut Wood and Metal Frames
- Canvas Stretching and Needlework
- Shadow Boxing
- Conservation/Preservation/Archival Framing
- Fine Art Packing/Shipping/Insurance

## EXPERIENCE

**Frame Land,** Honolulu, Hawaii, 1998–2001
*Manager*

In full charge of the main store and workshop. Reported directly to the owner. In charge of a staff of 25. Monitored inventory and served as buyer for all six stores (framing materials, fine art prints, workshop supplies, office supplies, promotional materials). Handled accounting, A/P, A/R, credit, and billing. This was a strong business, generating up to $62,000 each month from main unit alone.

Supervised shop and workshop. Provided technical expertise to all staff and retail customers. Handled specialty framing personally. Clientele was approximately 60 percent retail and 40 percent corporate and to-the-trade.

Provided V.I.P. service to interior designers, corporations, art consultants, galleries, and professional artists. Represented company to accounts. Handled entire sales/service cycle including setting up credit accounts and billing.

**Windward Community College Photography Department,** Kaneohe, Hawaii, 1997–1998
*Laboratory Technician*

Coordinated lab activities for 60 students. Provided technical expertise and consulting on technique. Monitored chemistry of developing agents. Maintained equipment. Ordered supplies, opened and closed the lab, ensured clean and safe environment.

## EDUCATION

**B.F.A., Art,** 1996
**Windward Community College**

# Louise Cunningham

lrc1972@aol.com

1234 Peachtree Lane
Savannah, Georgia 31419

Office: (912) 555-1616
Residence: (612) 555-1328

## EMPHASIS

### Real Estate Lending

Top producer. Major accomplishments in sales management and processing operations. Aggressive, entrepreneurial, systematic. Strengths: (1) providing leadership to a staff of top producers, (2) building close ties with major and minor players in the real estate community, (3) creating quality loan portfolios by originating preferred risks and through technical understanding of instruments and documentation.

## EXPERIENCE

Georgia Federal Savings & Loan, HQ: Atlanta                                    1998–Present
**A.V.P., District Loan Center Manager,** Savannah & Albany

Selected to take over this loan center, the largest loan center outside of the Atlanta metropolitan area, fourth largest in the entire branch system. Manage $200,000,000 annual production, plan $500,000 operating budget, direct staff of 35 (supervisors, sales reps, closers, underwriters, processors). Includes income property, construction and residential real estate lending, especially FHA, VA, FNMA, ARM, and jumbo instruments; all phases from origination through underwriting and funding.

*Accomplishments:*

- Recruited to run the most productive branch outside of Atlanta.
- Decreased turnaround time from 18 days to 7 days in first 6 months.
- Reduced audit errors to virtually nil in six months.
- Exceeded production goals every quarter.

**A.V.P., District Loan Center Manager,** Albany
*Accomplishments:*

- Achieved #1 market share with over $80,000,000 in funding per annum.
- Reduced turnaround time from 45 days to less than 15 in first six months.
- Served as interim manager for Macon office.
- Exceeded production goals every quarter.

Security Southern National Bank, HQ: Atlanta                                    1997–1998
**Manager, Real Estate Lending,** Valdosta
*Accomplishments:*
- Recruited to launch new office, reporting to Atlanta-based V.P.
- Developed and implemented sales/marketing campaign.
- Built new business from $0 to $5,000,000 in first six months.
- Ranked #1 in South Georgia and #2 statewide, with a brand-new office, in less than one year.

Northeastern Savings & Loan, Regional HQ: Macon                                 1994–1997
**Real estate Account Executive,** Macon
*Accomplishments:*

- Frequently ranked Top Producer in region, *consistently* ranked top 5 percent statewide, out of over 100 account executives.
- Also excelled in position as financial analyst, acting as budget and reporting liaison between four departments and senior management.

## EDUCATION

### B.S., Business Administration (Finance)                                     1994
Brigham Young University, Provo, Utah
- Dean's Scholarship
- Spanish (speak, read, write)

## Angelina Villanueva

1232 Calle Allegre del Sur
Phoenix, Arizona 85018
office: (602) 555-8743
private voice/fax/msg: (602) 555-6388
private e-mail: angel3@alumni.asu.edu

---

### STRENGTHS

**Staff & Operations Management**

Demonstrated talent for management of customer service operations. Skills include staff selection, training, and motivation; conscientious application of policies, procedures, and systems for inventory and cash control; budgeting and financial control in a corporate profit-center environment; community relations and promotions; computers.

### EXPERIENCE

**Burger Empire Corp.,** Phoenix, Arizona, 1999–Present
**General Manager**

Full profit and loss responsibility for $1 million unit. Train, motivate, and supervise staff of 35 including assistant managers and shift managers. Took a very proactive approach and turned this unit around from an F rating to top ranking.

- Dramatically improved unit gross and margin by tightening operations, retraining key staff, and improving food quality and speed of delivery.
- Improved staff morale; reduced turnover to record lows. Recently certified that 95 percent of staff has "above standard" level of performance.
- Successfully developed future managers. Two staff members promoted to assistant manager and one is now general manager of her own unit.
- Selected to serve as judge on Restaurant Manager Review Board. Also act as assistant market manager and district training manager.
- Participated in management training series, winning recognition as valedictorian of the PRO 2 class.
- Selected to give presentation on company's college recruiting video.
- Earned "Best in Region" in quality competition.
- Earned "Restaurant Manager of the Year," *Number one Nationwide!*

Currently seeking greater challenges and career growth commensurate with ability.

### EDUCATION

**M.B.A.** Candidate, Arizona State University, ongoing
Concentrations: **Management** and **Finance**

**B.S.B.A.** (Bachelor of Science in Business Administration), 1998
University of Denver, School of Hotel & Restaurant Management

**Architecture Major,** 1993–1995
University of Oregon, School of Architecture

*College Activities*

   Gold Key National Honor Society
   Sigma Pi Eta
   Chairperson, Area Standards Board

### PERSONAL

   References gladly provided on request, but please keep this information confidential at this time.

# KATE NICCOLLS

k5cents@netbase.net

1472 Telegraph Avenue #19
Berkeley, California 94706

Office: (510) 555-3115
Residence: (510) 555-2766

## STRENGTHS

**Sales . . . Marketing . . . Account Relations**

Senior level account manager. Direct interface with client company president and senior officers. Comfortable in highly competitive markets. Able to create client loyalty above and beyond the sales relationship. Dedicated to providing a high-quality performance for a high-quality product, service, or company.

## EXPERIENCE

**Gannett Outdoor**                                                              1998–Present
**Account Executive**

Sell local and national outdoor advertising space to media companies, advertising agencies and businesses with Northern California headquarters.

Set records for sales performance:
- #1 Top Producer as of first quarter 2000.
- Achieved 2000 target for *annual* sales in the *first quarter* of 2000. Consistently run 175 percent to 225 percent of company targets.
- Increased territory by 56 percent in first six months in position, and continued to achieve highest sales in history of this territory and highest profitability in last seven years.

Brought on board many new accounts. Samples:
- **Jenny Craig,** first time Gannett advertiser. Directed Sacramento test program, generating extensive free media publicity. Earned national rollout.
- **The North Face,** first-time Gannett advertiser, Bay Area, Denver, and New England placements.
- **KFOG,** first time Gannett advertiser, converting account from long-time relationship with major competitor.
- **Volkswagen,** won highly competitive bid, gaining a Gannett exclusive for local market. Worked closely with both company execs and agency account staff.

**Marketing Associate**

Originally hired as an account relations representative, entertaining client V.I.P.s when in the Bay Area and troubleshooting problem accounts.
- Promoted to account executive due to success in securing the **Corona Beer** outdoor campaign and due to repeated *requests of clients* to work with me as A.E.

**Evans/S.F.**                                                                     1998
**Account Executive** (managed largest account, 65 percent of total gross billings)

**Grey Advertising**                                                          1995–1998
**Assistant Account Executive** (Wyse and Consolidated Freightways)
**Media Planner** (earned promotion to account staff)

## EDUCATION

**Stanford University**
**B.A., Psychology**                                                               1994

Also: Graduate, Media School, Media Directors Council of San Francisco
   Graduate, PSS1 Learning Skills Sales Training Course
   Certificate, Marketing, Foothill College

# Matthew A. McMahon

1237 Lake Shore Drive, North
Chicago, Illinois 60610
(312) 555-1123
Mmgood@UI.edu

## objective

A drafting or design development position with a licensed architectural firm, with an opportunity to utilize and refine my skills and knowledge.

## skills

Technical drafting, plans, sections, interior and exterior perspectives, isometric and axonometric drawing, rendering, presentation construction documents, autocad, sketching, photography

Coursework in HVAC, lighting design, autocad, architectural engineering, architectural history. Experience as a design student in Europe.

Fluent in French (speak, read, write).

## education

**University of Illinois,** Champaign, Illinois
- Bachelor of Science in Architecture, 2000
- Design project selected for presentation to the East St. Louis Redevelopment Committee.

**L'Ecole d'Architecture et de l'Urbanisme,** Versailles, France, 1997–1998
- Dean's List. Straight A grade average.
- Gained rich understanding of variety of architectural styles.
- Studied design in foreign context. Expanded understanding of other cultures.

## projects

Hessel Park Christian Reform Church, Champaign
Student Residence Hall, Versailles
Museum for Theatre and Dance, Paris
Multiuse Commercial Facility and Theme Park, Discovery City

## employment

**Smith-Baxter Associates,** Chicago, Fall 2000
- Worked directly with the principal on design development project.
- Produced measured drawings of house, cafe, and warehouse.
- Organized drawing library and contributed to office management.

## portfolio

Portfolio, references, transcripts, and additional information provided on request.

## DEAN RODGERS

Rodgers Constructions Co.
874 Gerard Street
Mandeville, Louisiana 70448
154 Cayman Cove
Mandeville, Louisiana 70448

Office Direct Line: (504) 555-9616
Office General Line: (504) 555-9931
Mobile: (504) 555-3534
Fax: (504) 555-4074
Residence/Message: (504) 555-9142

**PROFILE**

**Over 30 years in trucking and transportation**

*Expertise:*
- Safety, Safety Programs, Driver Training
- Logistics

*Honors:*
- Over 3,000,000 miles without an accident.
- Outstanding series of awards and honors for safe driving from employers and from The American Trucking Association.

**EXPERIENCE**

**RODGERS CONSTRUCTION CO.**                 Mandeville, LA
**Trucking Supervisor/Safety Officer**           1999–Present

Hire, train, and coordinate drivers and owner/operators. Perform background investigations on drivers. Manage licensing records on drivers to insure proper credentials and status. Administer random drug testing program in compliance with state and federal laws. Represent company to state and federal regulatory authorities and insurance carriers. Maintain company safety programs and create new safety programs as needed. Maintain knowledge of state and interstate regulations impacting operations. Foster an environment of care and consideration for rules of the road and for the communities in which we operate.

Delegate daily assignments for owned trucks and leased trucks. Maintain all work records for trucks and drivers. Prepare payroll and lease payments for payroll department. Ensure driver discipline and compliance with company policies and regulations.

**CONTINENTAL BAKING CO.**                      Tulsa, OK
**Transport Driver**                              1990–1996

Drove approximately 600,000 miles accident free in Oklahoma, Kansas, Arkansas, Missouri and other states. Member, Safety Committee (appointed by management). Oriented and field tested new drivers. Numerous honors and awards.

**SAFEWAY STORES**                              Tulsa, OK
**Transport Driver**                             1986–1990

Drove four years accident free in Texas, Oklahoma, Arkansas, Missouri and other states.

**CHIEF FREIGHT LINES**                         Tulsa, OK
**Transport Driver**

Drove all combinations of tractor-trailer rigs over-the-road throughout Midwest, Atlantic Seaboard, Northeast, approximately 2,500,000 miles, all accident free, and including haz mats loads.

# Wade A. Stevenson

toolmon@lonestar.net

12770 Bellview Drive
San Antonio, Texas 78209

Telephone/Message:
(512) 555-5187

---

**STRENGTHS**

- **Restoration**
- **High-End Renovation & Remodeling**
- **General Contracting:** *Residential/Commercial/Industrial*

**PROFILE**

Over 20 years' experience, with last 9 years as project manager or super. Have pursued advanced understanding of multiple trades, especially carpentry, drywall, painting, surfacing and sealing, electrical, plumbing, tiling, and masonry.

Personally interested in working with a quality-oriented outfit.

**HIGHLIGHTS**

Restoration Design & Construction, San Antonio, Texas 1992–
**Project Manager** and **Superintendent**

Managed true, historical restorations of high-end residential properties and some commercial strips and buildings in and around San Antonio, especially in the King William neighborhood (all 100+-year-old homes). My personal specialty was kitchen and bath designs to update these homes in the historical styles. Carried projects from concept to completion, working with client, engineers, architects, subs, and suppliers.

*Sample Projects:*

- Project manager for the historical restoration of Southern Pacific Railroad Depot, including the renovation of the depot ceiling and a 16-foot diameter stained-glass window.
- Rebuilt to scale from old photographs a complete Alcatraz prison cell inside the Alcatraz Bar & Grill in Austin.
- Superintendent on $6 million restoration and rehab of 5000 s.f. commercial building into a mixed-use condo and retail/restaurant complex in downtown San Antonio.

Schouten Construction, Englewood, Colorado, 1986–1991
**Foreman** and **Lead Carpenter**

Troubleshooter for this government contractor, working to U.S. Army Corps of Engineers standards. Various short-term assignments nationwide with small crews of up to 10.

*Sample Project:*

- Took 6-man crew into King Salmon, Alaska, and built radar site with support buildings in 3-month building season.

**EDUCATION**

Chicago Technical College, Chicago, Illinois
**Blueprint Reading** and **Drafting**

- Plus dozens of product seminars over the last 25 years.

# Elizabeth Fleck

Telephone: (216) 555-1165
E-mail: ms24seven@earth.net

3721 Homestead Road
Cleveland, Ohio 44121

| | |
|---|---|
| **PROFILE** | Seeking a position as **accountant/bookkeeper** or **administrative assistant** with accounting/bookkeeping duties. Professional and articulate, qualified for client/customer interaction at all levels. |
| **SKILLS** | • Experience with small business accounting through financial statements and P&L. Includes G/L, A/P, A/R, P/R, balance sheet, trial balance, reconciliations, preparation of tax documents, and interface with CPAs. |
| | • Can self-train on new accounting/financial software, including data migrations. Effective problem solver. Capable of prioritizing and managing a heavy work flow without direct supervision. |
| | • Additional skills include general office, showroom reception, telephones, client interaction, and all administrative functions. |

**EXPERIENCE**

**Bookkeeper,** Archadeck                                                  (temporary) 2/01–6/01
• In full charge of P/R, A/P, A/R, financial statements, reconciliations, and trial balance for two business entities, the corporate HQ and one wholly owned franchise. Interfaced with 30 other franchise operations. Brought books from four months behind to current. Facilitated conversion from manual entry to fully computerized accounting for both businesses.

**Bookkeeper,** Miller Tomback Corp.                                          2/98–12/00
• Managed A/P, A/R, and subsidiary ledgers; prepared company P/R; prepared financials through P&L. Controlled the invoicing system from origination through posting to customer account. Computed billing and mailed statements. Formulated weekly aging reports for collection of overdue accounts. Completed cost accounting and profit calculations.

**Bookkeeper,** Bavarian Enterprises                                          9/95–1/98
• Posted to A/R and A/P journals, computed P/R, prepared P&L statement, analyzed employee sales, prepared W-2s. Brought books up from six months behind schedule to current. Developed daily checkout system that revealed shortages. Devised monthly sales analysis to compare sales-per-hour by employee.

**Full-Charge Bookkeeper,** Goodpasture, Inc.                                  8/97–1/98
• Set up all bookkeeping systems for this new business. Completed this project concurrent with above duties.

| | |
|---|---|
| **EDUCATION** | **B.F.A.,** Interior Design, Virginia Commonwealth University                5/94 |
| **ADDITIONAL** | Additional experience in **sales** and in **interior design.** Hobby: design/build/refinish furniture. Available for overtime and business travel as needed. |
| **REFERENCES** | Good recommendations available from all former employers. |

# RICHARD R. GLASTON

glastonr@fastweb.com

200 East Pearson
Chicago, Illinois 60611

Office/voicemail: (312) 555-4487
Residence/message: (312) 555-8749

## PROFILE

**Sales . . . Account Management . . . Sales Management**

Can plan and execute complex direct-sales programs, with emphasis on building business partnerships and generating customer loyalty. Strong background encompassing sales, distribution, marketing, merchandising, staff motivation. Comfortable with government relations and contract administration responsibilities in addition to sales.

## EXPERIENCE

**Gladstone Tire & Rubber Co.** 1996–Present
**Area Field Manager, Mileage Sales,** Chicago

Develop and service the major transit accounts based in Chicago, Detroit, Milwaukee, and Madison. Interact with contract administrators and purchasers in municipal governments and interstate trucking firms. Plan and conduct business development campaigns. Forecast sales and budget data for territory.

Prepare formal bids and proposals, including technical presentations and cost/benefit analyses. Negotiate details of contracts and agreements. Indirectly supervise a total of 33 service technicians.

- Assigned to territory to boost sales and turn around negative share trends. Increased monthly revenue from $250,000 to $400,000, a 60 percent increase in revenues in a mature market!
- Contributed to engineering and product development to meet customer specifications.
- Converted accounts from competitors; increased tire leasing activity; increased market share in a highly competitive market.

**Account Executive, New York City Transit Authority Account,** New York

Similar to above, servicing the largest single account in the nation, a $4.5 million relationship.
- Served as liaison between polymer engineers and upper management on product performance and testing; audited all account-generated reports.
- Successfully recruited, retained, disciplined, and motivated a staff of 28 technicians, with emphasis on labor relations that successfully avoided unionization.
- Coordinated distribution, including control of inventory parts and stock shipments.

**Management Trainee,** Akron

Training rotations through contract administration, sales, computerized sales planning and reporting, auditing, forecasting, and personnel management.

- Hand-picked from my training class to serve the NYC Transit Account.

**R. J. Reynolds Tobacco Co.** 1991–1995
**Sales & Merchandising** (full-time while in college)

| EDUCATION | | |
|---|---|---|
| | **Accounting,** University of Akron | 1992–1995 |
| | **Chemical Engineering,** Ohio State University | 1991–1992 |

**INTERESTS** Marathon runner. Health and sports enthusiast.

# Paul E. Davis

private e-mail: pd007@alumni.usc.edu

5417 Wilshire Blvd., Apt. 430
Los Angeles, California 90036

Office/voicemail: (818) 555-4775
Residence/fax: (213) 555-8629

## PROFESSION

**Public Relations** and **Corporate Communications**

Strengths include account management, concept development, media interface, event planning, and account team leadership. Skilled at encapsulating issues and presenting client issues in larger industrial/economic contexts. International orientation; bilingual French/English, proficient in German. Exclusive media contacts.

## EXPERIENCE

**Technaucracy Public Relations, Inc.,** Burbank, California, 1998–Present

Plan and implement full-scale corporate and product communications programs, including event planning, media relations, and collateral materials development. Account team of 6.

*Activities:*

- Conceive strategies and coordinate logistics for press conferences and national press tours.
- Schedule and monitor client product demonstrations at trade shows and press events.
- Manage ongoing client relations with key trade and business press and industry analysts.
- Coordinate development of design and copy for all promotional and collateral materials.
- Oversee client and agency relationships with designers, writers, photographers, other vendors.

*Accomplishments:*

- Landed client meetings with *New York Times, Wall Street Journal, Fortune, Venture, Business Week, Christian Science Monitor,* and many, many others.
- Solidified a "shaky" account by placing division chief's speech in 3 key publications.
- Contributed promotional strategy for rollout of 2 new products and oversaw presentation at Comdex trade show, resulting in favorable reviews by industry press and analysts.
- Discovered critical information about a client and canceled media tour, thereby saving client's and agency's reputations.

*Accounts:*

- Xerox Corporation
- CADAM/Lockheed
- Kyocera Corporation
- Cipher Data Products
- Fujitsu America
- Harris Corporation

**The Carmichael Group,** Los Angeles, California, 1997–1998
**Public Relations Intern** (legal, accounting, and architectural clients)

**The Oregonian,** Portland, Oregon, 1995–1996
**Reporter,** Business Features

## EDUCATION

**B.A., Journalism,** University of Michigan, Ann Arbor, 1995

*Honors:*

- Alpha Gamma Sigma (scholastic honor society)
- Alpha Mu Gamma (foreign language honor society)

# Stephan Davies

832 Pacheco Drive, Apt. B
San Jose, California 95132

mr.geni@hyperusers.worldlink.net
Residence voice/msg/fax: (408) 555-9210

**PROFESSION**   **Mechanical Designer** and **CAD Specialist**

**SKILLS**
- CAD/CADD/AUTOCAD, Computervision CAADS-4X, CALMA, and others for mechanical and electrical design (2-D, 3-D, and modeling over time).
- Solid knowledge of engineering math: analytical geometry, algebra, trig, as well as applied math for physics.
- Experience in a range of aerospace, biomedical, process automation, machine tool and production engineering projects.
- Qualified to serve as integral member of engineering team, contributing to all states from conceptual design to final drawings.

**EXPERIENCE**
Litton Industrial Automation, Alameda, California, 2–12/2000
**Mechanical Designer** (Contract Services, Inc.)
- Design layouts and design details for mechanical assembly; detailed manufacturing drawings for fabrication.
- Solved alignment and lockdown problems related to reflective mirrors and support structure used in optical laser-beam data-verification system.

FMC Ground Systems Division, San Jose, California, 8–12/1999
**Mechanical Designer** (Butler Services Group)
- Modification of mechanical parts used in hull of FAADS-LOS ground defense vehicle using Computervision CAADS-4X.

Target Therapeutics, San Jose, California, 10–12/1999
**Mechanical Designer** (Contract Services, Inc.)
- Design and detail drawing of extrusion device used for fabrication of high precision plastic catheters used for heart-vessel and brain-vessel repair.

Edible Technology, Inc., Sunnyvale, California, 5–8/1999
**Mechanical Designer/Drafter** (Contract Services, Inc.)
- Mechanical drawings of operating parts for an automated pizza-vending machine.

ZETA Labs, Sunnyvale, California, 7/1996–2/1997
**Electrical/Mechanical Design Drafter** (Contract Services, Inc.)
- Layout of mechanical microwave housings, mechanical layouts, electrical schematics, wiring diagrams, and trace layouts.

Calspan Corp., NASA/AMES Research Center, Moffett Field, California
**Drafting Specialist,** 7/1995–6/1996
- On-site drawings of Alperin vertical injector engine, wind tunnel modification drawings, wind tunnel pressure test probe drawings.
- Also: designed fixtures for wind tunnel calibrations.

**EDUCATION**
**A.A., Mechanical Design Drafting,** DeAnza College, Cupertino
**Scientific/Technical Program,** NASA/AMES Research Center
**AUTOCAD Training,** The Copper Connection, Inc.

**ADDITIONAL**
Seeking long-term, permanent position. Willing to start in contract or project capacity to prove skill and value. U.S. Citizen. Availability: Immediate.

# Sharon Mason

doc2b@prs.com
937 Brunswick Street
New London, CT 06320
(401) 555-8100

---

| | |
|---|---|
| **SKILLS** | **Operations Analysis** |
| | **Procedures Design & Documentation** |
| | **Staff Training** |
| | |
| **TECHNICAL** | **Radiological Engineering** |
| | **Environment Engineering** |
| | **Industrial Hygiene** |

**EDUCATION**

**Ph.D.** candidate, **Physics**                    beginning fall 2001
University of Connecticut, Storrs, Connecticut

**B.S., Physics (Nuclear)**                    1998
Arizona State University, Tempe, Arizona

| | |
|---|---|
| Nuclear Physics | Optics |
| Electricity & Magnetism | Electromagnet Fields |
| Thermal & Statistical Physics | Chemistry & Biology Core Series |

**Certificate, Radiological Controls for Engineers**     1999
U.S. Navy

**EXPERIENCE**

Department of Defense, Naval Shipyard, New London, Connecticut
**Nuclear Engineer**                    1998–Present

- Design and incorporate radiological controls into technical work documents. Write radiological control procedures into each project document based on project-specific parameters.
- Serve as lead engineer of maintenance teams. Direct the removal and decommissioning of heavily contaminated equipment.
- Develop and deliver staff training on (1) reactor plant systems, (2) quality control of operations, (3) radiological exposure controls.
- Serve as emergency control officer for the designated personnel processing area under F.E.M.A. plan.
- Maintain understanding of exposure, radioactive material transport, radioactive liquid transfer.
- Maintain skills in radiological and environmental testing.

**AWARD**      Received commendation from superior and cash bonus performance award.

**ADDITIONAL**      Employment while in college: sales, math tutor, child counselor. Available for travel or relocation as needed.

# Michael Dodd

md33@pacific.net
1825 Union Street, #4
San Francisco, California 94123
Residence/Message: (415) 555-2643
24-Hour Message: (800) 555-7011, ext. 27

## EXPERTISE

### Sales / Marketing / Promotions / New Business Development

Proven performer with demonstrated ability to gain account loyalty and win preferential treatment for products. Personable and enthusiastic, able to organize and focus the efforts of others. Strengths include:

- Educating account management and floor sales staff on product.
- Creating special events and public relations activities.
- Designing promotional and incentive programs.
- Following through on organizational details.
- Maintaining a positive, fun image.

## EXPERIENCE

**Napa Valley Wines & Spirits Co.,** Napa, California, 1998–Present
**Account Executive,** San Francisco

Selected to manage 50 high-profile accounts in downtown San Francisco. Built close, personal relationships with key management in each account, creating a genuine bond of friendship and mutual purpose.

*Accomplishments:*
- Designed, coordinated, and managed on-site wine tastings and luncheons. Created innovative promotions such as casino night, winery tours, and other account relations activities. Supported accounts by attending, organizing, or sponsoring special events, fundraisers, house parties, and similar.
- Obtained account participation in maximum number of supplier or wholesaler programs. Facilitated participation by serving as liaison between all parties. Followed through on every account to ensure service on the sale.
- Used former career in F&B to gain buyers' trust due to understanding of their businesses. *Created increased sales for accounts,* which leads to loyalty and greater participation in upcoming promotions and programs.
- Increased wine sales by 75 percent over prior year.
- Increased liquor sales by 14 percent over prior year.

*Sample Accounts:*
- Splendido
- Postrio
- Bistro Roti
- Bix
- Corona Bar & Grill

- Masa's
- Bentley's Oyster Bar
- Big 4
- Kuleto's
- Grand Hyatt & other major hotels

**PRIOR**
**Bar Manager,** 565 Clay Restaurant, San Francisco
**Bartender,** Modesto Lanzone's, Opera Plaza, San Francisco
**Bartender,** Scomas Restaurant, San Francisco

## TRAINING & EDUCATION

**Beringer Wine Seminar** (3-day professional seminar in the winery)
**Berringer Train-the-Trainer Seminar**
**Robert Mondavi Tasting Seminars**
**B.S., Geology,** James Madison University, Harrisonburg, Virginia

# Leander M. Hamilton II

23 Pinehurst Circle
Denver, Colorado 80235

lmh-hotsauce@aol.com
Telephone/message: (303) 555-2296

## PROFILE

**F & B Operations** (multiunit or major operations, including resort and hospitality)

Background of proven success in entrepreneurial restaurant/F&B endeavors. Combination of M.B.A. financial skills, staffing and operations expertise, and marketing/promotions savvy. Experience features timely involvement with trendy, formula restaurants, as well as grounding in highly controlled, corporate fast-food operations. Strengths include:

– Concept, image, and menu development
– Design of policies and procedures
– Training of management-level staff
– Training of operations-level staff
– Quality assurance (top-to-bottom, front-to-back)
– New product development
– Operational control (waste control, food and labor cost control, inventory and cash control)

Other strengths include extensive experience with international kitchen and work crews and knowledge of international foods. "Kitchen proficiency" in both French and Spanish.

## EDUCATION

Golden Gate University, San Francisco, California
**M.B.A., International Management**

Culinary Institute of America, Hyde Park, New York
**Certificate, Professional Chef Training & Kitchen Management**

California State University, Sonoma, California
**B.A., English,** and **B.S., Political Science** (double degree)

## MANAGEMENT EXPERIENCE

**The Palm**, Barbados, West Indies
**Consultant**

1999–2000

Start-up consultant on this new restaurant. Contributed to all stages: concept and image development, restaurant design, construction supervision, equipment layout and installation, menu development.

– Hired and trained original staff. Trained chef and asst. chef on recipes.
– Succeeded with extensive negotiations and lobbying with local government officials to win necessary regulatory approvals.
– Completed business launch under projected budgets.
– Achieved positive cash flow for the owner and turned over the operation as scheduled. Excellent recommendation available.

*continued . . .*

<u>**Taco Bell Corporation**</u> (PepsiCo), Sacramento, California                          1996–1999
**General Manager**
    Assigned the highest volume restaurant in the Sacrament region.
    – Achieved 24.5 percent cost of sales, bottom-line operating profit in excess of 32.25 percent.
    – Managed first unit in region to break $1 million in sales.
    – Raised quality assurance scores from the F to C range to a quad B.
    – Facilitated R&D for new product roll out.
    – Appointed to the Manager Review Board.

<u>**Leander M. Hamilton Associates**</u>, San Francisco, California                        1993–1994
**Restaurant Consultant**
    – **Clark's**, London, England. Start-up consultant. Set up kitchen and menu. Trained initial chef
      and kitchen staff.
    – **Polo Lounge**, Bangkok, Thailand. Marketing consultant. Developed marketing plan to attract
      more tourists and American clientele. Revised bar list.
    – **The Carlisle Club**, Barbados, West Indies. Redesigned bar operations at popular nightclub.

<u>**Mill Restaurant**</u>, Coconut Grove, Florida                                        1991–1992
**Manager**
    Hired to turn around negative sales trend in established restaurant with good name recognition but
    uneven operations.
    – Increased profit margin from negative to 28 percent.
    – Reestablished relations with better hotel and tour operators.

<u>**Le Parite Restaurant**</u>, Coconut Grove, Florida                                    1991–1992
**Manager**
    – Achieved a ★★★ rating, one of the very few in the state.

## COOKING EXPERIENCE

**Guest Chef**, Narsai's, Kensington, California
**Sous Chef**, Commercial Club, San Francisco, California
**Line Cook**, Scandia Restaurant, Los Angeles, California

## ADDITIONAL

Additional experience in Europe, West Indies, Southeast Asia, Caribbean

———————

**MENUS ON REQUEST**

# Ruth Ann Waters

raw@lawserv.ss.org
1351 Seminole Street, #6
Miami, Florida 33133
(305) 555-5946

**OBJECTIVE**

**Word Processing / Secretarial / Clerical / General Office**
- Efficient, good-natured, good reputation with all former employees
- IBM and Mac expertise in all common office suites
- Basic accounting/bookkeeping
- Fast learner
- Accurate

**EDUCATION**

Miami/Dade Community College, Miami, Florida
**Associate of Applied Arts** (Major: Legal Office Management)          expected 9/2001

Hialeah High School, Miami, Florida
**Diploma** (Honor Roll)          6/1995

**EXPERIENCE**
(while student)

United States District Court, Miami, Florida
**Secretary**          2000–present
- File memos, find and copy cases from law books, type correspondence, maintain office supplies, enter cases on computer. Successfully perform all duties in an atmosphere where accuracy and the ability to follow detailed orders is critical. Cleared three-month backlog in three weeks.

Host Systems, Miami, Florida
**Office Assistant**          1999
- Entered data on Macintosh computer. Ensured accuracy and completeness of data to be entered. Maintained clean and well-organized office. Also served as the office courier.

Lechter's Housewares, Miami, Florida
**Assistant Manager** (official title: Second Key)          1999
- Managed store in absence of manager and assistant manager. Opened and closed registers. Balanced daily receipts. Ordered some merchandise. Sold and supervised. Earned rapid promotion.

Cruise Time, Miami, Florida
**Office Assistant**          1998–1999
- Maintained account information on PC: accounting, billing, and client information. Managed monthly invoicing. Answered incoming phones. Handled all errands as a courier.

Alcott & Andrews, Miami, Florida
**Stocker**          1997

Ross Department Stores, Miami, Florida
**Floor Sales Associate**          1995–1996

# Special Styles, More Tricks

Some industries have evolved their own distinctive résumé styles. If your résumé is not in the appropriate style for your industry, then you will look like an outsider, *even if you have the right experience.* For instance, believe it or not, airplane pilots and ship captains have their own style of résumé. In this chapter, we will investigate a few of the more common style variations.

In some cases, the industry has a particular way of handling the information, and sometimes it just has a particular look that may be hard to describe but easy to show. Immediately following the narrative of this chapter are full-size samples of résumés that illustrate the points mentioned below. You may want to refer back and forth between the narrative and the samples to really get a feel for the different styles.

## Legal                                    Samples: Andrew Baxter Clay, Barbara J. Damlos

Attorneys' résumés are distinctive, but legal secretaries, paralegals, legal office administrators, and others in the legal field use standard résumés and should follow the résumé instructions elsewhere in the book.

If you are an attorney, you should never put an objective on your résumé; you *are* your objective. A border-to-border line under the address, universal in other résumés, is rare. Profiles are also rare, but if you have a specialty you can list it with a heading like one of these three examples:

| | |
|---|---|
| **EXPERTISE** | Corporate Taxation |
| **EMPHASIS** | Employment Law |
| **INTEREST** | Environmental Law |

Always write *v.* instead of *vs.* and *judgment* instead of *judgement.* List "Member, State Bar of California," not "Member of the Bar, State of California," as bar membership is technically extragovernmental. Understatement is definitely the preferred tone, brevity the rule. It's also a good idea to put something interesting somewhere on these résumés to keep them from looking like ten thousand others. Note the nonlegal job on Andrew Baxter Clay's résumé. Include journal publications and published opinions if available, as shown on the Barbara J. Damlos résumé.

## Finance                               Samples: Elizabeth Whitney-Wingrove, E. Edleff Schwaab

Finance résumés look a lot like attorneys' résumés, especially on the East Coast. This style may or may not have a profile, and small type and expansive white space contribute to the distinctive look. Most jobs in this sector are gotten by personal introduction and word of mouth, so résumés are noticeably less flashy than in other industries. On the West

Coast, finance résumés tend to look more like regular business résumés. Most commercial bankers, insurance executives, and others in fields related to finance should design their résumés with a standard profile and appearance.

**Curriculum Vitae** (medical, scientific, academic)   Sample: Joshua D. F. Gordon, M.D.

A curriculum vitae, or "C.V." as it is commonly known, is a highly stylized type of résumé. Education always comes first, and job descriptions can be extremely brief or nonexistent. Full listings of publications are a common feature, and this style can run on for pages if poorly arranged by the candidate. Although there are many variations, Dr. Gordon's C.V. is a classic example. Note the human interest listing at the bottom, to distinguish this résumé from hundreds of others. For more examples of academic, medical, and scientific curricula vitae, see my book, *Asher's Bible of Executive Résumés.*

### Advertising                                                     Sample: Mary McHale

Advertising résumés always list clients and account teams on which the candidate has served, and little else. Ironically, the résumés of copyrighting geniuses are just plain lists of accounts and campaigns. At the entry level, you will want to apply your eloquence to a skills-based résumé as fully described in prior chapters, but once you have any experience at all, simply listing your accounts is the standard style. Public relations résumés are similar to advertising résumés. Prominent listings of accounts are standard, but so is featuring your skills and abilities more fully. Compare Mary McHale's résumé in this chapter with the public relations résumé from Paul E. Davis in the previous chapter.

### Acting and Modeling                                           Sample: Andrea Tipton

Acting résumés are simply tables of performances. They are designed to fit onto the back of an eight-by-ten photograph, usually a head shot. The younger and less experienced the actor, the more training, church plays, and nebulous listings will be featured. As their careers progress, actors list only their best and most recent work, but always on an eight-by-ten sheet of paper. Acting résumés never list an actor's address. It will show the phone number only, or the phone number and address of the actor's agency. Modeling résumés are almost identical, just listing shoots, products featured, and usually the name of the ad agency thrown in for good measure. Height and weight are standard listings, but race is never discussed.

### Art, Music, TV, and Film                                      Sample: Bruce Golin

Studio musicians, TV and film people, cartoonists, and those with similar talents often have careers that consist of an unending series of projects, or "credits." Bruce Golin's is an example of a credits-based résumé, which is a good solution for this type of background.

### Artist's Bio                                                    Sample: Martha Paulos

An artist's bio is a short biographical statement about her life and philosophy of art. This type of bio is particularly useful, as it can be displayed in a gallery along with the artist's work. When applying to galleries, a bio like this would be paired with a credits-style résumé showing training and a list of prior shows and awards. No address or phone is on the bio when it is hung at a show, as all contacts should be made through the gallery.

### Consultant's or Speaker's Vita                                Sample: Nathaniel A. Robertson

Similar to an artist's biography, consultants' and speakers' vitae are third-person promotional pieces. These vitae are designed to be used in marketing a firm, justifying a firm's high fees, and introducing the principals at speaking engagements. Most speakers' bureaus write vitae like this on every speaker they represent. Note that this style is most clearly *not* to be used for getting a job. For more examples of vitae, see my book, *Asher's Bible of Executive Résumés.*

### "Shuffle the Deck of Cards" Résumé     Sample: Barbara Hermann

Ms. Hermann's résumé is the trickiest one in this book. Note how the repeated use of the subheading "duties" allows all the work histories to be written in the present tense. With the dates omitted, every single one of these jobs is interchangeable. They can be rearranged and re-sorted endlessly! We dropped and re-sorted jobs completely out of order to create this presentation and several others. I would not recommend this for most candidates, but this client reported that she got *tons* of interviews and multiple offers with this résumé. Simply amazing.

### Recent College Grad—No Work History     Sample: Danaelle Watkins Bell

This candidate has never worked for pay one day in her life, yet following the guidelines in this book, she has put together a compelling first résumé. (On technical grounds, this résumé does not belong in this chapter, because it does not show any new techniques. However, if I did not point out the candidate's complete lack of paid work experience, you probably would not notice anything unusual about this résumé at all.) Compare this example with the one for Josephine Juddley on p. 55, which highlights student employment.

### Functional Résumé     Sample: Jeanine Kjömpedahl

A functional résumé, also known as a "topical résumé," has the candidate's duties and accomplishments *from all jobs* lumped together under categorical headings such as "Accounting" or "Human Resources," then lists all the employers and job titles at the bottom, with or without dates. The sample featured in this book is a modified functional résumé, because I have distilled my client's skills and built a traditional profile for her on top of the functional categories. For support positions, this style will still get interviews and jobs. As a matter of fact, this résumé gets this client a new job about twice a year.

### Housecat     Sample: Ernie

This résumé was written by my associate Susan Hall. These last two examples prove that with a little imagination you can write a good résumé for *any* background and *any* objective.

**Sylvia** by Nicole Hollander

# Andrew Baxter Clay

Baxter@NYC-Home.com

10 Downing Street, Apt. 2T
New York, New York 10014

Office (212) 555-6800
Residence: (212) 555-8395

Member, State Bar of New York, admitted 1998

## EDUCATION

*legal*
HARVARD LAW SCHOOL, Cambridge Massachusetts
**Juris Doctorate,** June 1998
Activities: Editorial Staff, *Journal on Legislation*
Law School Council: Committee to Renovate the Student Union
Ames Moot Court Competition

*college*
NORTHWESTERN UNIVERSITY, Evanston, Illinois
**Bachelor of Arts,** History, 1995
Honors: Phi Beta Kappa
Hearst Award (highest department GPA)
Graduated with honors for senior thesis analyzing the relationship between popular culture and public policy in the context of the Iran-Contra hearings.

*preparatory*
CAIRO HIGH SCHOOL, Cairo, Illinois
Honors: Valedictorian
State Debate Champion

## EXPERIENCE

*legal*
ASCHER, ELIASSON & RHEIKHART, New York, New York
**Attorney,** September 1998–Present
Member of trial team for the $2.1 billion Texoil pollution coverage litigation. Managed numerous smaller matters. Prepared and argued motions. Defended depositions. Currently carrying the major responsibility for a multimillion-dollar commercial dispute between a corporate insured and its insurer.

ASCHER, ELIASSON & RHEIKHART, New York, New York
**Summer Associate,** July–August 1997
Prepared summary judgment motion. Researched and drafted memoranda for corporate and litigation matters. Observed depositions. Received permanent offer.

ISHAM, LINCOLN & BEALL, Chicago, Illinois
**Summer Associate,** June–July 1997
Researched and drafted memoranda for numerous cases. Received permanent offer.

HIGGS, FLETCHER & MACK, San Diego, California
**Law Clerk,** summer 1996
Researched and drafted memoranda for personal injury and business litigation. Drafted settlement conference brief, orders, and trial briefs for an attorney malpractice case.

*nonlegal*
BAUMAN FARMS, Reese, Michigan
**Farmer,** summers 1993, 1994, 1995
Operated 200-acre farm on profit-sharing basis. Drove and maintained all equipment. Made crop marketing decisions. Earned full tuition for junior and senior years of college, and first year of law school.

# BARBARA J. DAMLOS

damlos@waltweb.com

1800 Greenwich Street
San Francisco, CA 94132

Office: (415) 555-6451
Residence: (415) 555-1636

**EXPERIENCE**

**MISCIAGNA & COLOMBATTO,** San Francisco, California
**Partner**                                                    1995–Present
Insurance defense litigation in the areas of insurance coverage, insurance bad faith, personal injury, and products liability. Drafted appellate writs.

Published opinions:
*Bodenhamer v. Superior Ct.* (G.A.B.)(1996)178.Cal.App.3d.180
*Bodenhamer v. Superior Ct.* (St. Paul)(1997)192.Cal.App.3d.1472

Primarily responsibility for trial preparation. Assisted lead counsel in four-month trial of insurance bad faith case.

**TOLPEGIN, IMAI & TADLOCK,** San Francisco, California
**Law Clerk**                                                    Fall 1994
Directed discovery of toxic tort litigation. Research and drafted pleading, motions for summary judgment, and discovery requests.

**BIANCO, BRANDI & JONES,** San Francisco, CA
**Law Clerk**                                                    5/1993–5/1994
Researched issues in unfair competition, trade secrets, product liability, and insurance bad faith. Reviewed personal injury and malpractice cases.

**HANCOCK, ROTHERT & BUNSHOFT,** San Francisco, California
**Law Clerk**                                                    Summer 1992
Researched legal issues in bankruptcy proceedings, construction actions, and insurance coverage cases involving asbestos-related claims.

**HANCOCK, ROTHERT & BUNSHOFT,** San Francisco, California
**Paralegal**                                                    7/1990–8/1991
Assisted in preparation of two major construction cases for trial.

**EDUCATION**

**UNIVERSITY OF SAN FRANCISCO SCHOOL OF LAW**
**Juris Doctor**                                                    1994
Law Review
Semi-Finalist, Advocate of the Year competition, Moot Court Honors Program
First Place Award, Oral Advocacy, Moot Court Competition

**PUBLICATION**

*The Duty of Good Faith—More Than Just a Duty to Defend and Settle Claims,* 14 Western State University L.Rev.209(Fall 1996)

**AFFILIATIONS**

Member, State Bar of California
California Trial Lawyers Association
Bar Association of San Francisco

(Please keep this application confidential at this time)

# Elizabeth Whitney-Wingrove

600 Quincy Street, #110
Boston, Massachusetts 02125

whitney-wingrove@wallstreeters.com
24-hour voice/message/fax: (617) 555-8311

---

**EXPERIENCE**

*financial*   **M. P. Handel & Co., Inc.,** 1995–Present
Boston, Massachusetts

**Institutional Equity Sales Trader,** 1997–Present

Service 30 major institutional accounts. Solicit trades, execute trades, develop client relationships, distribute research product, sell investment ideas. Recent concentration has been educating clients on our foreign products, including settlement operations and capital commitment services. Completed intensive research project on international program trading.

Selected to take over the entire account base of a senior partner, a total of 76 accounts. Completed two months advanced training in New York. Currently travel approximately 30 percent to key accounts and company offices in New York, Philadelphia, Washington, and London.

**Sales Assistant to Research Salesperson,** 1995–1997

Assisted in sales and client services related to analysts' reports on 15 selected industries. Included direct client interaction at all levels, planning/hosting/coordinating meetings and social engagements for institutional investors. Provided administrative and technical support. Coordinated with New York and Washington offices. Retained through several mergers: M. P. Handel, Smythe & Holden, Rowe & Pitman.

*prior*   **Lanier Business Products, Inc.**
Chicago, Illinois
**Senior Sales Representative,** Corporate Accounts
   *Top producer*

**Weather Tamer, Inc.**
Chicago, Illinois
**Assistant Marketing Director**

**Huntington Industries, Inc.**
Chicago, Illinois
**Cost Analyst**

**Bullocks Wilshire**
Los Angeles, California
**Senior Assistant Buyer**

**EDUCATION**   **M.B.A.,** Finance, Boston University, 1993
**B.S.,** Fashion Retailing, Institute of Design, Chicago, 1988

**CREDENTIALS**   **NASD Series 7** (Series 63 pending)

**REFERENCES**   References and additional information provided on request. Please keep this application confidential at this time.

# E. Edleff Schwaab

mr.finance@telnet.com
1250-F Piccadilly Place, White Plains, New York 10601
(914) 555-5820 (home), (800) 555-2406 (work)

| | | |
|---|---|---|
| **EDUCATION:** | NEW YORK UNIVERSITY, New York, New York | |
| | **M.B.A., Finance,** *summa cum laude* | 1993 |
| | SYRACUSE UNIVERSITY, Syracuse, New York | |
| | **B.S., Accounting,** *magna cum laude* | 1990 |
| **CREDENTIAL:** | **CFA Candidate** | |
| | Level I (passed) | 1999 |
| | Level II (results pending) | 2000 |
| | Level III (anticipated) | 2001 |

**EXPERIENCE:** MAHAN, ROMANSKI & O'CONNOR, INC., New York, New York
**Portfolio Manager/Securities Analyst**　　　　　　　2000–Present
Co-manage a publicly traded, diversified high-income mutual fund. Developed the original investment strategy, prepared marketing material and selected investments for the fund. Performance has led to an eightfold increase in assets under management in the fund to $8 million in the first 7 months. This fund is currently performing third out of 86 high-yield funds as ranked by Lipper.

Also prepare general investment analysis for this firm, which has $1 billion total assets under management. Conduct fundamental research, communicate with management and sell-side analysts, and assess economic and industry trends. Select and monitor investments in the following sectors: banks, S&Ls, insurance, airlines, aerospace, machinery and equipment, diversified companies, convertible bonds, and high-yield bonds.

EMPIRE FINANCE SAVINGS BANK, Riverhead, New York
**Senior Investment Analyst**　　　　　　　　　　　1998–1999
Co-managed $100 million high-yield bond portfolio. Recommended investment decisions. Prepared written and oral presentations to CFO, CEO and chairman on strategies and ideas. Sole liaison to management of companies under investment, sell-side analysts, and traders.

TPFM&C (a Towers Perrin Co.), New York, New York
**Senior Financial Analyst**　　　　　　　　　　　　1994–1998
Developed models, projected cash flows, and valued a range of potential mergers, acquisitions, divestitures, LBOs, and alternate capital structures. Developed and analyzed long-range financial and business plans.

Developed methodologies and financial models to analyze 9 acquisitions and 9 divestitures worth over $1.5 billion, which were approved and consummated according to plan.

ASHLAND OIL, Pittsburgh, Pennsylvania
**Senior Financial Budget Analyst**　　　　　　　　　1990–1994
Developed, analyzed, and interpreted corporate operating and capital budgets. Supervised 3 financial analysts.

**ACTIVITIES:** Competent Toastmaster (CTM), Toastmasters International
New York Marathon (last eight years)

## JOSHUA D. F. GORDON, M.D.

**Curriculum Vitae**

820 Mill View Lane
Los Altos Hills, California 94022

jdfgmd@aol.com
Telephone/voice/pager (24/7): (415) 555-0132

**SPECIALTY**      **Anesthesiology**

**CREDENTIALS**

| | |
|---|---|
| Board Eligible, American Board of Anesthesiology | 2000 |
| Basic Life Support Instructor | 2000 |
| Advanced Cardiac Life Support | 2000 |
| Diplomate, National Board of Medical Examiners | 1997 |
| Federal Licensure Examination | 1996 |
| Medical License, State of California | 1995 |
| Medical License, State of Ohio | 1994 |

**EXPERIENCE**

**Staff Anesthesiologist**

| | |
|---|---|
| Santa Clara Valley Medical Center, San Jose, California | 2000–2001 |
| Pacific Presbyterian Medical Center, San Francisco, California | 2000–2001 |
| Sonoma Valley Hospital, Sonoma, California | 2001 |
| Seton Medical Center, Daly City, California | 2001 |

**TRAINING**

**Research Fellowship** (blood bank and liver transplant anesthesia)      2000
University of California, San Francisco

**Residency** (anesthesiology)      1997–2000
University of California, San Francisco

**Internship** (internal medicine)      1996–1997
University of California, San Francisco

**EDUCATION**

**M.D.,** College of Medicine      1996
University of Cincinnati, Cincinnati, Ohio

**A.B.,** Biochemical Sciences      1992
Princeton University, Princeton, New Jersey
   Thesis: *Studies on a Deletion Mutant from a Recombination Bacteriophage Library*

Three Advanced Levels (physics, chemistry, biology)      1988
Twelve Ordinary Levels      1986
Harrow School, Harrow-on-the-Hill, England

*continued . . .*

Joshua D. F. Gordon, M.D.  C.V./page 2

## RESEARCH

*ARTICLES:*

"The Pharmacokinetics of Vecuronium During Liver Transplantation in Humans." J. D. F. Gordon, M.D.; J. E. Caldwell, F.F.A.R.C.S.; M. C. Prager, M.D.; M. L. Sharma, Ph.D.; L. D. Gruenke, Ph.D.; R. D. Miller, M.D. *Anesth. Analg. 2000;* 70: S432 (abstract, presented at the IARS 64th Congress, Honolulu, Hawaii, March 13, 2000).

"Vecuronium Plasma Concentrations During Orthotopic Liver Transplantation in Humans." J. D. F. Gordon, M.D.; J. E. Caldwell, M.B.Ch.B.; M. C. Prager, M.D.; M. L. Sharma, Ph.D.; L. D. Gruenke, Ph.D.; D. M. Fisher, M.D.; N. Ascher, M.D.; Ph.D.; R. D. Miller, M.D. (submitted).

"The Effect of Aprotinin on Intracranial Pressure and Cerebral Edema in Rabbits with Galactosamine-Induced Acute Liver Failure." J. D. F. Gordon, M.D.; M. C. Prager, M.D.; S. F. Ciricillo, M.D.; M. Grady, B.A. (submitted).

"A Comparison of HTLV-1 Seropositivity in Orthotopic Liver Transplant Recipients Before and After Routine HTLV-1 Screening." J. D. F. Gordon, M.D.; E. Donegan, M.D.(in preparation).

*ADDITIONAL:*

"Fibrinolysis During Liver Transplantation," in association with Dr. Marie Prager, Department of Anesthesia, Dr. Marc Shuman and Dr. Larry Corash, Department of Hematology, UCSF, 2000.

"Analysis of Lymphocyte Subset Variations Associated with Liver Transplantation," in association with Dr. Elizabeth Donegan, Director of Blood Bank, UCSF, 1990.

## AFFILIATIONS

| | |
|---|---|
| American Society of Anesthesiologists | 1998–Current |
| International Anesthesia Research Society | 1998–Current |
| California Society of Anesthesiologists | 1998–Current |
| Northern California Anesthesia Society | 1998–Current |

## COMMUNITY SERVICE

| | |
|---|---|
| Volunteer, Animal-Assisted Therapy Program, San Francisco SPCA | 1999–Current |
| Instructor, Basic Life Support, American Red Cross, Southwest Ohio Chapter | 1995–1996 |

## PERSONAL INTERESTS

Interested in therapeutic aspects of animal-human relationships, especially as related to illness recovery and geriatrics. Hobbies include Weimaraner dogs and violin. Certified Grade VII (Final) "with distinction" in violin, Board of Royal College of Music, London.

# Mary McHale

adgirl@earthlink.net

615 Marina Way
Sausalito, California 94040

Office: (415) 555-2000
Residence: (415) 555-7166

## EXPERIENCE

FOOT CONE AND BELDING, San Francisco, California, 1990–Present
**Senior Broadcast Buyer / Spot Account Manager**

*Place over $15 million per year in broadcast time for such clients as:*

| | | |
|---|---|---|
| • Mastercard | • Albertsons | • Long John Silvers |
| • California Raisins | • C&H Sugar | • Dreyers Ice Cream |
| • Levi Strauss | • Colgate-Palmolive | • California Milk Advisory Board |
| • Mazda | • Adolph Coors | • Pacific Bell/Pacific Telesis |
| • Universal Studios | • Hughes Airwest | • Supercuts |
| • Citicorp | • Orion Pictures | • Mattel |
| • Clorox | • Payless Shoe Source | • Ashton-Tate |
| • ARCO | • Farmers Insurance | • Alaska Tourism |
| • Eddie Bauer | • First Interstate | • Bertschi Books |

*Buy for up to 47 markets simultaneously. Have bought over 200 rated markets in the U.S. and Canada, with emphasis on:*

| | | |
|---|---|---|
| • San Francisco | • Seattle | • Sacramento |
| • New York | • Dallas | • Kansas City |
| • Atlanta | • Phoenix | • Tampa |
| • Cleveland | • Philadelphia | • Las Vegas |
| • Cincinnati | • Honolulu | • Minneapolis |

*Skills include:*

- Analyzing, negotiating, purchasing, maintaining, and monitoring radio and TV buys. Additional skills include post analysis, client contact, and training of assistant buyers.
- Negotiating radio and TV sports sponsorship packages for clients, including TV and radio schedules, promotions, and merchandising programs.
- Serving as liaison with buyers, planners, account management, and clients, including contact with FCB regional offices.

*Prior experience provides well-rounded background:*

- Assistant media buyer (one year), commercial production account coordinator (two years), print production coordinator (two years)

## EDUCATION
**Holy Names College,** Oakland, California

## REFERENCES
References and client accolades citing skill and professionalism provided on request.

# ANDREA TIPTON
## (SAG, AFTRA)

Frederick & Templeton Agency, Inc.
6608 Hollywood Boulevard, Hollywood, CA 90028
(213) 555-8506 {in New York, call (212) 555-6100}

## DATA

| | | |
|---|---|---|
| Height: 5'7" | Hair: Blond | Ages: 23–25 |
| Weight: 115 | Eyes: Blue | Lang: Italian, Polish, Greek |

## FILM

| | | |
|---|---|---|
| *When Harry Met Sally* | Waitress | Rob Reiner, Dir./Castle Rock |
| *Zelda* | Zelda | Paul Scott Reuter, Dir./ NYU Student Film |
| *Bye Bye Budapest* | Mrs. Borbas | Margeaux Wasommer, Dir.; WSU Student Film |

## THEATRE

| | | |
|---|---|---|
| *The Snow Queen* | Snow Queen | Long Beach Players/Long Beach, CA Deborah La Vine, Dir. |

*"A visual delight—a female Mr. Spock,"* Heffley, L.A. Times
*"A beautiful, regal Snow Queen,"* Warfield, Drama-Logue

| | | |
|---|---|---|
| *The Woolgatherer* | Rose | New Studio Theatre/Detroit, MI |
| *A Midsummer Night's Dream* | Titania | Mullady Theatre/Chicago, IL |
| *Uncommon Women* | Rita | Mullady Theatre/Chicago, IL |
| *Lysistrata* | Corinthian | Mullady Theatre/Chicago, IL |
| *Rattlesnake in a Cooler* | Ellen | Detroit Repertory/Detroit, MI |
| *Who Killed Richard Cory* | Mistress | Fourth St. Playhouse/Royal Oak, MI |
| *Quail Southwest* | Kerra | Fourth St. Playhouse/Royal Oak, MI |
| *The Late George Apley* | Lydia | Henry Ford Theatre/Dearborn, MI |

## COMMERCIALS

List upon request

## STAND-UP COMEDY

| | | |
|---|---|---|
| At My Place | 1990 | Santa Monica, CA |
| Igby's Comedy Cabaret | 1990 | Los Angeles, CA |

## TRAINING

| | | |
|---|---|---|
| The Groundlings | Improv | Los Angeles, CA |
| Judy Carter | Stand-Up Comedy | Los Angeles, CA |
| Greg Dean | Stand-Up Comedy | Los Angeles, CA |
| Lawrence Parke | Scene Study | Los Angeles, CA |
| Loyola University | B.A., Drama, 1986 | Chicago, IL and Rome, Italy |
| Lodz Film School | Acting | Lodz, Poland |
| Kosciusko Foundation | Acting | Warsaw, Krakow, Wroclow, Poland |

# Bruce Golin

4366 Monroe Avenue, #107
Studio City, California 91604

answerman@trivia.com
Telephone/pager (24/7): (818) 555-0575

## PRODUCER/CO-PRODUCER

### STRENGTHS

- Twelve years in television — great record for on-time and on-budget
- Good communicator with writers, talent, crew, production and post-production techs
- Strong on directing/shooting inserts and second-unit filming

### CREDITS

**Virtual High School** (New Syndicated Series), The Arthur Company, 2000–Present
   Position: Producer
   Executive Producer: Burton Armus

**All Monica — All the Time** (CBS), Comedic Production, 1998–1999
   Position: Associate Producer
   Executive Producers: Tom and Dick Smithers—Producer: Ken Kragen

**Jenny McCarthy's Closet Tapes** (CBS Special), BRB Productions/Peep Pictures, 1997
   Position: Production Manager
   Executive Producer: Steve Binder—Production Executive: Howard Malley

**No Diets Needed** (USA for Africa), Golin-Malley Productions, 1995
   Position: Stage Manager
   Executive Producer: Steve Binder—Producers: Craig Golin, Howard Malley

**Knight Rider** (NBC Series), Universal Television, 1994–1996
   Position: Associate Producer
   Supervising Producers: Burton Armus, Bruce Landsbury

**Simon & Simon** (CBS Series), Universal Television, 1992–1994
   Position: Assistant Associate Producer
   Executive Producer: Phil DeGuere—Producer: Richard Chapman

**Legends of the West** (ABC Special), Marble Arch Productions, 1991
   Position: Production Coordinator
   Producer: Eric Lieber

**The Gambler** (CBS Movie of the Week), Kenny Rogers Productions, 1990
   Position: Production Coordinator
   Producer: Ken Kragen

**The Lily Tomlin Show** (NBC Special), Tomlin Productions, 1989
   Position: Production Coordinator
   Producer: Rocco Urbisci

### EDUCATION

   **Premed,** University of California, Los Angeles

## Martha Paulos

Montreal
Canada

**"I like snakes; they're flexible and
come in all colors." —*Botero***

Martha Paulos is a Montreal artist known for her sculptures of animals and plants, all of which she calls paintings. Her brightly colored representations exhibit a pervasive sense of humor and a strong sense of the unusual in the mundane. The emotive impact of her works is initially humorous, hiding a more concealed cynicism that adds a depth unknown to many young artists.

A full decade of formal study behind her, Ms. Paulos is working in the tradition of American and Mexican naive and primitive art. Secondary influences include Flemish portraiture and Italian Renaissance painting.

Ms. Paulos produces unavoidable, interesting sculptures of cacti, people, dogs, snakes, and other animals, and has recently begun to produce a series of houses. Having focused on nearly lifesize pieces, she is now moving toward developing arrangements of her independent characters into total environments.

With five years of serious exhibitions, Ms. Paulos is an emerging and prolific artist, and has already won a significant award for one of the dog sculptures, a yellow pit bull with a snake in his mouth. She has pockets of aficionados throughout Canada and the United States, shows regularly in New York, and is just now beginning to attract the attention of serious collectors.

As a thoroughly modern artist, Ms. Paulos is refreshingly accessible. Now at the Lumina Gallery, Quebec City, P.Q. (418) 555-1942.

**Robertson & Associates**

Attorneys-at-law
3810 Melrose Place, Suite 1500
Los Angeles, California 90029
(213) 555-4964 or (213) 555-1713

---

### Nathaniel A. Robertson
#### BIOGRAPHY

Nathaniel A. Robertson is a graduate of Stanford University and the University of California at Berkeley (Boalt Hall) School of Law. He is a member of the ABA, the NBA, and the CBA and is licensed to practice before all California State Courts, Federal District Court, and the U.S. Court of Appeals. Mr. Robertson is well known in legal and business circles in both Northern and Southern California. He has been described by at least one media source as a "major force in West Coast litigation."

Mr. Robertson is currently the principal of Robertson & Associates, a law firm specializing in legal research and representation concerning matters of banking, securities, commercial credit and tax law, general business and contract litigation, professional liability, personal injury, product liability, appellate services, and such related services as negotiations, advocacy memoranda, and representation to tax, government, or regulatory authorities.

In addition to heading his law practice, Mr. Robertson serves as a private consultant to banks and fiduciary entities. He provides advisory services, structuring, and oversight for a wide range of transactions and agreements, for both corporations and financial institutions. This includes projects for such institutions as the European Industrial Development Bank and more routine assistance to such entities as the Arbuckle Consulting Group, the renowned Southern California venture capital firm.

Prior to starting his firm, Mr. Robertson was the founder and executive director of the Western Legal Research Institute at Stanford for seven years. WLRI is a legal think tank and support firm providing quality research, writing and analysis to private practitioners, corporate counsel, and attorneys in government. Mr. Robertson has built a team of dynamic young attorneys around this new concept, and this "law firm's law firm" gained quick recognition as both innovative and highly resourceful. WLRI has continued to grow and has been touted as the model of a new breed of legal services firm.

WLRI provides litigation, research, and analysis in the areas of administrative law, automobile injury, banking, civil procedure, civil rights, commercial law and bankruptcy, constitutional law, contracts, corporate law and antitrust, criminal law and procedure, eminent domain, energy, environmental law, family law, labor law, pension benefits, copyright and trademark, personal injury, product liability, real property, securities, torts, trusts, wills and estates, and workers' compensation.

Mr. Robertson's earlier career spans assignments as research attorney for the California Supreme Court and research clerk/fellow/extern for Public Advocates, Inc., Honorable Justice Frank M. Newman, Pacific Gas and Electric Corporation, National Aeronautics and Space Administration, Legal Aid Society of Alameda County, and the U.S. House of Representatives Subcommittee on Equal Rights.

# Barbara Hermann

2310 Rio Grande Street
Houston, Texas 77040

maskedgirl@tallstories.com
Telephone/message (713) 555-3125

## PROFILE

**Administrative Assistant**
- Career secretary, administrator, front and back office staffperson. Over 15 years in office environments. Extensive computer experience. Can self-train.
- Skilled in all general office: word processing, data entry, light bookkeeping, clerical, invoicing, writing/editing documents, and correspondence.
- Also skilled as front office and/or executive assistant: screening calls and visitors, routing mail and deliveries, maintaining calendars, and managing travel arrangements.

## HISTORY

Gulf Coast Salvage & Recycling, Houston, Texas
**Office Administrator**

*Duties:*

- Handle all administrative, secretarial, and clerical support for plant. Manage large cash fund and accounting records. Prepare weekly/monthly production reports, data entry.

The Sharper Image, Houston, Texas
**Authorizations Representative,** Credit department

*Duties:*

- Verify credit card data for phone and mail orders. Communicate with customers and banks.

Monadnock Building Associates, Dallas, Texas
**Administrative Assistant**

*Duties:*

- Receptionist for the management office of this high-rise building. Handle lease administration, accounts receivable ledger, correspondence, and secretarial duties.

Latch Management Services, Dallas, Texas
**Receptionist**

*Duties:*

- Front desk management for this management consulting firm. Requires advanced interpersonal and client relations skills, in addition to general office.

Blue Cross of Texas, Galveston, Texas
**Clerk/Typist/Customer Service**

*Duties:*

- Clerk/typist, third-party liability clerk, customer service representative for Hospital and Professional Liaison Unit and Correspondence Unit.

## EDUCATION

**Certificate,** Secretarial Studies, Mrs. Caldwell's Business College, Tulsa, Oklahoma

# DANAELLE WATKINS BELL

3736 Lakeland Avenue                                                   dwb@diana.com
Minneapolis, Minnesota 55422                                           (312) 555-4972

---

**INTERESTS**          **Editing, Writing, Research**

**STRENGTHS**
- Technical command of the English language: grammar, syntax, semantics, spelling, punctuation.
- Experience in copyediting and proofreading according to *The Chicago Manual of Style.*
- Significant experience in primary research; very resourceful at finding data and developing primary and secondary sources.
- Wide-ranging knowledge of history, politics, cultures, and science.

**EDUCATION**          University of Colorado, Boulder
*degrees*              **B.A., History**                                December 2000
- Graduated magna cum laude.
- Thesis: *Cinderella Learned to Fly: An Examination of Women Aviators of WWII.*

                       Shady Side Academy, Pittsburgh, Pennsylvania
                       **Diploma**                                      May 1996

*activities*           National Outdoor Leadership School
                       **Leadership Training**                          Spring 1998
- Baja California survival and ecology trip.

                       University of Pittsburgh, Pennsylvania
                       **Semester at Sea**                             Fall 1997
- Traveled around the world on the U.S.S. Universe.

*symposia*             **Magazine Writers' Symposium**                  Fall 2000
                       **Aspen Writers' Conference**                    Summer 2000

**EXPERIENCE**         University of Colorado, Boulder                  1999–2000
                       **Researcher** (senior research project)
- Collected data from across the country on women aviators of World War II. Researched primary and secondary materials in USAF National Archives and other government sources.
- Found and interviewed women veterans. Visited USAF Academy to record views of women cadets today.
- Wrote 80-page academic thesis.

                       University of Colorado, Boulder                  Fall 1999
                       **Instructor's Assistant**
- Selected by the head of the Astrophysics Department to serve as student aide.

                       University Hill Elementary School, Boulder, Colorado   Fall 1999
                       **Tutor**
- Reading and writing tutor.

**TRAVEL**
- Bicycled to New Zealand; traveled in Australia, Thailand.          Spring 2001
- Traveled in Europe.                                                Spring 1999
- Bicycled through Great Britain.                                    Summer 1998
- Kayaked in Baja California.                                        Summer 1997

# Jeanine Kjömpedahl

129 Windview Terrace Place, #108
Albuquerque, New Mexico 87123

Telephone / Message:
(505) 555-0174

**CAREER DIRECTION**
Seeking **Secretary/Administrative Assistant/Office Manager** position utilizing a strong combination of analytical, interpersonal, and leadership skills.

**TECHNICAL SKILLS**

| **IBM PC** | **Keyboarding** (65 wpm) | **Excel** |
| **Mac** | **Transcription** | **Lotus** |
| **Word** | **Editing** | **Quicken** |
| **WordPerfect** | **Proofreading** | **Quickbooks** |

**EDUCATION**

**Certificate, Office Applications**                                                    2000
Southwest Community College, Albuquerque, New Mexico
• Advanced training on all common office suites.

**Certificate, Office Technology,** certified *with honors*                 1998
Control Data Institute, Albuquerque, New Mexico
• Maintained 95 percent GPA, award for "Outstanding Attendance."

**Economics** and **Business Administration**                              1991–1995
University of New Mexico, Albuquerque
• Completed 3½ years toward B.S. in economics while working full time.

**EXPERIENCE**

**Administration & Office Management**
• Prepared and modified large cost proposals, including multiple-variable contract modifications using Excel for engineering contracts.
• Worked as only office, administrative, and bookkeeping person on major construction site, including control of large petty cash fund on site.
• Posted accounts receivable, maintained general ledger through trial balance. Researched and reconciled all accounts.
• Supervised computer and clerical staff in Look Back and TAA medical research, tracing former patients using national databases such as TRW.
• Consistently demonstrated telephone and organizational skills.

**Interpersonal & Leadership**
• Contacted former patients and informed them of potential exposure to AIDS virus. Demonstrated caring and compassionate manner.
• Achieved high volume of sales in straight-commission sales positions.
• Coordinator and chair for "Employee Day."
• Made collection calls for a major jeweler.
• Received *numerous* letters of commendation from associates about my work.

**Technical**
• Strong technical/analytical aptitude. Experience as a laboratory technician, hospital equipment technician, and in other medical-oriented assignments requiring mathematical/statistical skills.

**HISTORY**

| | |
|---|---|
| **Secretary/Office Manager,** Mark Diversified Contracting, Inc. | current |
| **Administrative Assistant (PR),** Veterans Memorial Hospital | 1999 |
| **Administrative Clerk,** Carpet Connection | 1998–1999 |
| **Equipment Technician,** Veterans Memorial Hospital | 1997–1998 |
| **Sales Associate,** Standard Shoe Store | 1995–1996 |
| **Administrative Specialist,** Thames Temporary Agency | 1993–1994 |

# ERNIE

Alley #3
Corner Market & Broadway
Megaopolis, New York 10012

## OBJECTIVE

Long-term position as **Housecat**

## QUALIFICATIONS

- Omnivorous. Strong rodent-control capabilities.
- Excellent nonverbal communication skills. Highly developed purring mechanism.
- Affectionate. Adaptable. Rare feline willingness to follow established guidelines.
- Proven stud potential.

## EXPERIENCE

**BARNCAT,** Westchester Estate, New York                    March 1998–May 2000

Ensured day-to-day rodent and small animal control for two-story, 35,000 sq. ft. barn.

- Consumed average of over 5 rodents per day.
- Achieved 37 percent reduction in barn swallow population.
- Awarded feline leukemia inoculation after 1 month of service.
- **Earned in-house privileges for outstanding service and deportment after only 2 months on the job!**

**ALLEYCAT,** Wilshire Boulevard, Los Angeles, California       November 1996–February 1998

Successfully maintained territorial boundaries of 4 sq. block area in notoriously competitive and dangerous location. Developed high degree of proficiency in urban survival, hunting, and scavenging skills.

- Honored by co-cats for consistent expertise in maneuvering safely and adroitly through heavy skateboard, auto, and roller-skate traffic.
- Known sire of at least 77 feline litters over 9-month period.

## EDUCATION

**Certificate, Feline Deportment**                                    January 1997

TOM & JERRY ASSOCIATES, Hollywood, California

(1-year intensive with Tom of famed "Tom & Jerry" partnership)
**High Honors**

## REFERENCES

Enthusiastic recommendations provided on request.

# Scannable, Internet, and HTML Electronic Résumés

A résumé-writer friend of mine, Walt Schuette, thinks the drawings on the cave walls at Lascaux are nothing less than the first résumés. They show the painters' prowess in hunting, just the kind of information a potential employer would need to know 15,000 years ago. Résumés have been evolving ever since. Letters of introduction served as résumés in the last century and part of this, then the barest list of employers and dates, and now the sales-oriented document you've been learning to write in this book.

The latest developments in this continuum are scannable and Internet résumés. The optimum approach is to write the best résumé you can, using the advice provided so far, and then *modify* that document to work as a scannable or Internet résumé. Here's how.

> Wait a minute! Let me say right here that if you don't get this chapter, skip it and skip the next one and keep going. Don't become bogged down in technology gobbledygook if it's not your thing. Get on with the book, get on with the job search, and get on with your life. *No stumbling blocks allowed.*

## Scannable, Internet, and HTML Résumés *are* Electronic Résumés

Scannable and Internet résumés have certain features in common. They are used to create an electronic database of your skills and abilities that is then indexed by search engines. So you write your electronic résumé for a search engine, not for the eye and heart of a human.

For this reason, electronic résumés are very noun-based, not verb- or adjective-based. Search engines will not be impressed with everything you "created" or how "proactive" you were. They are looking for nouns like *cost accounting* and *biotechnology*. Most keywords employers use to search résumé databanks are nouns, and highly specific nouns at that.

You need to consider the search tools AND, OR, NEAR, and NOT, as well. Often employers search for general terms to describe the field AND some specific software package, brand name, or former employer, for example: *administrative assistant* AND *PowerPoint*, or *computational chemist* AND *MatLab* AND *Java*, or *computational chemist* AND (*Dow* OR *Dupont*).

Since search engines have not achieved the level of artificial intelligence yet, they are easily fooled. If you live on Spanish Lane and are involved in research into possible medicinal derivatives of Spanish moss, many search engines will jump to the conclusion that you speak Spanish, as well. This can work for you or against you.

If your graduate business degree is a master of science in management, you will be disqualified from all those searches specifying an MBA. So go through your exciting, written-for-a-human-being résumé and add in clarifying nouns, in parentheses, if need be, so that it is idiotproof. Here is one example:

Krannert Graduate School of Management (Graduate School of Business)

Purdue University, West Lafayette, Indiana

MS, Management (Master of Science in Management)

(equivalent to MBA, M.B.A., Master of Business Administration)

You see that being redundant is not only okay in an electronic résumé, it is in fact the *best way for you to present critical information.* Anticipate the most common and obvious ways to present important aspects of your background, and then list them *all.*

Obviously, you can stack the deck in favor of hits by spamdexing, using wording that you think a potential employer will search for. For example, in your profile or objective, you can say, "Interested in biotechnology and cost accounting, especially with such quality companies as Genentech, Dow Pharmaceutical Sciences, XOMA Corporation, Genelabs Technologies, Bio-Rad Laboratories, and Abgenix."

Get it?

**Do not spamdex!** Your goal is to get humans to look at your résumé for all those positions for which you are fully qualified, not to get spam hits where you look like a jerk.

Many electronic résumés have a keyword list at the top, but I recommend you leave your powerful profile alone and have your keyword list at the bottom of your electronic résumé, even if it repeats a lot of the information presented elsewhere in the same document. **Keep the top of your résumé designed to impress a human,** who will hopefully eventually see it. The search engine will be happy to read all your résumé, I assure you, whereas the human will start at the top, expecting to be impressed right away. Remember, with humans it's win or lose in the first ten lines.

Some people point out somewhere in their electronic résumé, "Printed version provided upon request via fax or overnight courier." If you've advanced to the human-review level, you don't want to be stuck with an ugly, clunky printout from an electronic version.

The length of an electronic résumé is virtually irrelevant. Don't worry if it is three or four pages long. The computer won't care. Start your résumé with the word *resume* on the first line, without accents and all by itself, and end your résumé with this last line, "End resume," on the final line, all by itself. Do not number or otherwise mark page breaks, and remove any page numbers and page headings from your printed version.

### Scannable Peculiarities

Start every line on the left margin. Don't center *anything,* not even your name. Having multiple right and left margins confuses scanners. Remove all graphics, lines, borders, bullets, underlining, bold, and italics. Do not right justify. Separate paragraphs with a double return and headings with a triple return. Computers interpret space as a change in topics. Take bulleted tables and lists and turn them into comma-delimited sentences. For example, take this:

- Accounting
- Payroll
- Tax Filings
- Cost Accounting
- Management Accounting
- Special Studies

and turn it into this:

Accounting, cost accounting, management accounting, payroll, tax filings, taxation, special studies, management studies.

This is the most conservative way to prepare a résumé for scanning, but scanners are becoming much more talented. Most can already read italics and bold, though underlining is sure to throw them into fits.

Many companies scan all the résumés they save from the round file, fancy layouts and all. They don't scan in perfectly, but they're still indexable. I recommend that if you are sending in your résumé unsolicited to a major company, you provide them with *two* versions of your résumé: one for humans and one for scanning. Take a yellow temporary stick-on note and label the unattractive scannable version: "Scannable version."

Be sure to add a keyword list in which you throw in the kitchen sink, pipes and faucets and all.

## Internet and HTML Peculiarities

The problem with generalizing about Internet and HTML résumés is that they are constantly mutating. For starters, HTML is the programming language of the Internet, so HTML résumés *are* Internet résumés, but not the only kind.

Résumé databanks accept input in many forms—ASCII, rich text format, Word, WordPerfect, HTML, direct entry in a Web-page window—some of the above or all of the above. Even if you don't know HTML from Slobavian, all major word processing programs can now translate your résumé into/out of/between any and all of these formats. The best rule for submitting Internet résumés is to *follow the instructions of the site or person accepting the résumé.* I assure you that busy headhunters and employers will not spend much time trying to unlock or decipher your file if it arrives in a nonpreferred format. Additionally, many systems are fully automated and are programmed to just dump any files that don't load properly.

Whether you can include layout and design, bold and italics, and so on will depend on the format you submit your document in. Most Internet résumés are just exactly like regular printed résumés. They have the same words in the same order, but HTML résumés can be written in a new way, where portions of your résumé are hyperlinked to expand upon request or have a "go to" command sending the reader to another location in a document that is basically otherwise linear. The trend is away from using hyperlinks just to jump around in a document and toward using hyperlinks to expand into various levels, or rooms off a hallway, if you will.

HTML résumés can be submitted to anyone with an Internet browser. They are definitely going to be the résumé of the future, and I recommend you build one now. You can start with an HTML programming guide and software package. Word processors will translate some basic designs, but you'll want to get more sophisticated than that as soon as you can. For example, if you use HTML you can put your keywords in the <META> field. Most search engines are set up to scan this field, and it does not display in the browser (if you open up the source code, however, you can see it). The <META> field is part of the <HEAD> field, following the </TITLE> and looks like this:

> <META Name="description" Content="resume, applications engineer, intranets, Java, Sun, cost planning, WIP, systems administration, Novell, Microsoft CNE, html coding, version control, software related engineering">

Do *not* submit at HTML résumé with a picture. Any major employer will immediately freak out, as accepting pictures of job applicants exposes them to litigation. Your own home page can have a picture, however, and you can call your reader's attention to your home page.

By the way, take a good look at your home page. Many employers search for an applicant's home page, whether she mentions it or not. If you have a home page full of erotic poetry and diatribes against an ex-spouse, you might want to clean that up, mothball it for the duration of your search, or remove search keys that have your name associated with them.

As mentioned elsewhere, do not use your business e-mail for job-searching purposes, and when you do get a personal account, be careful about your account name. What would you think if you got a résumé from hotbabe@whatever.com, monkeyboy@whatever.com, or sexxfrk@whatever.com? People *do* read e-mail addresses, so act like a grownup. You can go back to being a sexxfrk after you land a new position.

Finally, don't get too hung up on this whole Internet and scannable résumés topic. **You get jobs by talking to people.** Don't hide behind technology.

Following are two versions of the same résumé, one scannable and one a crude B&W printout of the first screen of an HTML résumé. The gray words would be hyperlinks to additional information.

After looking at these examples, be sure to check out the next chapter. It's full of good links for job searching.

Resume

Kimberly Haase
haase-on-fire@logon.net
37 East 9th Street, Apt. 7-R
New York, New York 10003
Office: (212) 555-3276
Residence: (212) 555-7914

PROFILE
Buyer and merchandiser specializing in high-end fashion, fine watches, fine jewelry, and gifts. Effective communicator and interface between senior management, buying office, sales floor, vendors, and V.I.P. customers. Experienced supervisor, motivator, trainer. Good leadership ability, including setting a high standard for service. Able to coordinate and focus the efforts of others. Also: advanced analytical skills, including "what if" modeling of buying and merchandising data. Software and brands in keywords list at bottom of resume.

EXPERIENCE
Tarbells on Fifth
New York, New York
2000–present
Title: Merchandiser
Prepare and execute seasonal plans for $12.3 million in sales of fine watches at the flagship store, Tarbells on Fifth, 22 branch Tarbells stores in New Jersey and Connecticut, and fine jewelry and watch counters inside another 18 stores under co-op agreements. Coordinate advertising and promotions, negotiate with vendors, coach and motivate sales staff in high-end gift sales. Provide conceptual direction to the line.
Contributions:
Created 122 percent increase in sales at co-op counters, and 15 percent increase in sales at Tarbells stores in a flat market for luxury gift items. Designed the merchandising planning system using $ALES ANALY$I$ software. Eliminated six unprofitable profit lines and developed three new lines representing $1.8 million in first-year business.

Marlissa et Jacque
New York, New York
1999–2000
Title: Buyer
Prepared and executed seasonal sales plan for $10.2 million in business at 24 stores. Analyzed and reported on sales flow. Negotiated with vendors, coached floor sales staff, used ZIPPER software to analyze profitability and flow-through on multiple factors (SKU, designer, style, color, size, store, etc.).
Contributions:
Developed a home fragrance business that ran 100 percent increase. Personally directed store merchandising and educated staff on product. Coordinated and promoted trunk shows. Designed new personal shopper programs. Appointed mentor in M&J's Rising Stars (management training program, management development program, staff development).

Macy's
New York, New York
1998–1999
Title: Sales Manager, Department Sales Manager
Trained, developed, and motivated a staff of 19 sales associates. Ensured compliance to store policies and procedures. Oversaw combined sales of $1.2 million per month.
Contributions:
Designed a travel shop within the department, eventually duplicated in all stores. Developed a microwave "cooking school" delivered on-site at area college and university campuses with discount coupons tracing 900 percent ROI.

Other experience:
Macy's
New York, New York

Title: Selling Supervisor
China/Crystal Department

John Haase & Associates, Retail Consultants
Beverly Hills, California
Title: Training Assistant

City of Beverly Hills, Personnel Department
Beverly Hills, California
Title: Human Resources Intern

EDUCATION
University of Southern California
Los Angeles, California
B.A. (Bachelor of Arts), Organizational Behavior / Industrial Psychology, 1997

University of Paris, France — Sorbonne
Paris, France
Studies in French language, culture, and history, Fall 1996

LANGUAGES
Fluent in French, some basic understanding of Spanish, Portuguese, and Italian. Successful with a sophisticated, international clientele.

KEYWORD LIST
Fine jewelry, fine watches, high-end gifts, gift items, co-op agreements, housewares, bath shop, fragrance business, $ALES ANALY$I$, SALES ANALYSIS, ZIPPER, zipper, RET-X, StoreWatch, Store Watch, Windows 2000, VaporWare, Windows 98, Windows 95, Windows NT, DOS, MS DOS, MS Office Suite, Corel Office Suite, WordPerfect 8.0, WordPerfect 7.0, WordPerfect 5.2, WordPerfect 5.1, Lotus Notes, Excel, spreadsheets, Lotus 1-2-3, IBM PC, Mac, iMac, RET-X workstation, chain stores, specialty stores, consignment sales, gold, diamonds, estate jewelry, estate sales, staff development, executive development, sales training, motivation, skills enhancement, pay-for-performance, pay for performance, stepped discipline, workers compensation, employment law, Tiffany's, Macy's, Shreve & Co., Saks Fifth Avenue, Neiman Marcus, Maxfield's, Piaget, Tag Haur, Cartier, Blanc Pin, Rolex, Raymond Weil, Jean-Paul Gaultier, Comme des Garcons, Issey Miyake, Yohji Yamamoto, Matsuda, Romeo Gigli, Giorgio Armani, Verri, Claude Montana, Thierry Mugler, Byblos, Paul Smith, Katharine Hamnett, Donna Karan, Calvin Klein, Karl-Lagerfeld, Jil Sander, Norma Kamali, Stephen Sprouse, Chantal Thomasss, Jean-Charles de Castelbajac, Moschino, Dolce Gabanna, Mizrahi, Giorgio di sant Angelo, Emanuelle, Michael Kors, G-Gigli

End resume.

# Kimberly Haase

haase-on-fire@logon.net
37 East 9th Street, Apt.7-R
New York, New York 10003

Office: (212) 555-3276
Residence: (212) 555-7914

## PROFILE

Buyer and merchandiser specializing in high-end fashion, fine watches, fine jewelry, and gifts. Effective communicator and interface between senior management, buying office, sales floor, vendors, and V.I.P. customers. Experienced supervisor, motivator, trainer. Good leadership ability, including setting a high standard for service. Able to coordinate and focus the efforts of others. Also: advanced analytical skills, including "what if" modeling of buying and merchandising data. Software and brands in keywords list at bottom of resume.

## MANAGEMENT SKILLS

Honors / Awards
Merchandising
Store / Department Management
Opening Staff / New Stores
Forecasting / Analysis
Software / Systems
Training / Staff Development

## BRAND KNOWLEDGE

Watches
Men's Fashions
Women's Fashions

## EXPERIENCE

Tarbells on Fifth, **New York, New York**                                           2000–present
**Merchandiser,** Fine Watches, Gifts, $12.3 million business.

Marlissa et Jacque, **New York, New York**                                           1999–2000
**Buyer,** Men's & Women's Fashion, $10.2 million business.

Macy's, **New York, New York**                                                       1998–1999
**Sales Manager, Department Sales Manager,** $14.4 million combined business.

**Macy's,** New York, New York
**Selling Supervisor,** China / Crystal

**John Haase & Associates,** Beverly Hills, California
**Training Assistant**

**City of Beverly Hills, Personnel Department,** Beverly Hills, California
**Human Resources Intern**

## EDUCATION

**University of Southern California,** Los Angeles, California
**B.A.** (Bachelor of Arts), **Organizational Behavior / Industrial Psychology**        1997
More on college activities.

**University of Paris, France — Sorbonne,** Paris France
Studies in **French** language, culture, and history                                  Fall 1996
More on travel.

## LANGUAGES

Fluent in **French,** some basic understanding of **Spanish, Portuguese**, and **Italian.**
More on experience with international clientele.

KEYWORD LIST

# Directory of Career-Oriented and Job-Search Web Sites

## CHAPTER 14

The World Wide Web is a great place to search for a job or to gather information about all that is involved in the job-search process. There are thousands of Web pages on the Net providing career and job-search-related information, including résumé guidance, writing a cover letter, how to perform well in an interview, how to actually find a job, general information on different career fields, and so on to the nth level. Most important for the jobseeker is the tremendous number of sites where you can search for openings and post your résumé so employers can search for you. This directory is composed of those sites with job-search and résumé-posting capabilities that are used most frequently by both jobseekers and employers. It attempts to point out the unique aspects of each site, if there are any, so that you can go to the ones that may cater more to the type of job or career resources you are looking for.

Once you begin searching, you will soon discover that there is a general structure to the majority of these sites. On a most basic level, you can do a job search, post your résumé in the site's database, and browse through a few pages of career-related information. Each site takes off from there, with different options and variables that will shape your search. Some sites allow you to search only by location (sometimes with a limited number of places to choose from), while others allow you to pick the zip code you want to work in, salary preferences, occupational category, the skills you have, full-time or part-time preferences, and more.

Before you begin filling out a large and detailed search form, however, try at least one broad search. Ask for all the jobs in California, say, or all the jobs for nurses. Looking at that list will give you clues about how deep and current the database is. If you do a broad search and see that there are only five jobs listed in your state, there is no point in going back to the long search form and filling in more detail. The more you know about a database, the better you will be able to manage your search. If there is a *browse* feature, explore that for a few minutes before investing greater effort. Sometimes there is nothing wrong with your search parameters, just insufficient material in that particular database for your particular needs.

Generally speaking, searching in those sites with a greater number of search variables tends to result in a greater number of job listings. While this seems counterintuitive, the fact that the site has such complicated search parameters is a result of the fact that it has more listings in its database in the first place.

When you post your résumé to a site, you may be able to cut and paste your own, or you may have to simply fill out a qualifications questionnaire the site has composed for you. Filling out a site's forms is incredibly time consuming, doesn't allow you to display much individuality, and may leave out some of your most important skills and experiences. Try to spend your time (résuméwise) first on those sites allowing you to cut and paste your own résumé. By the way, do *not* spend all day on line, blocking your incoming telephone lines. Get another phone line for your Internet access, or a message server that records incoming calls while you're on line.

Some sites charge you to post your résumé. I receive widely varying reports from candidates about the utility of various sites and have come to this general conclusion: If you are an executive, most of the executive-only sites *do* charge, just to cut down on traffic and maintain their elite feel. If you are looking for six-figure jobs, expect to pay subscription fees. If you are not an executive, there are plenty—and I do mean plenty—of free sites that I hear great things about, so if your budget is tight, pursue these only. Before paying any site, visit a career-search message board and post a query about the site. If you don't hear good news from other candidates, skip it.

There is one last thing to be aware of. Each site has a different résumé-posting period. Some sites list you as a "new" candidate every time you change something in your résumé, so frequent modifications are a good idea. Some keep your résumé for thirty days, others a year, and a few indefinitely. If you plan on posting to a site that will keep your material in the public domain for a longer period of time, *make sure* you understand their procedures for making changes, deleting, or replacing your posting. Some sites won't let you make any changes at all, and you may resent that at a later date, if you keep getting calls long after you're happily ensconced in a new life.

Other than that, online posting is a great way to let your experience be known.

Not all of these sites are for job searches. A few are merely informational, providing guidance in the job-search process. The whole first section of the directory has been dedicated to these sites. They can be very helpful when you're starting out, to get basic information on electronic job-search techniques. Browsing the information may get you accustomed to the online environment, as it compares to ripping through the Sunday newspaper employment section. Additionally, many of these sites do contain links to other sites that have job-search databases or more specialized job-search and career information. They are worth checking out.

One last warning: The Web is so named for a reason. It is easy to get tangled in its threads, and at times you may feel lost, overwhelmed, and frustrated. Remember that there are plenty of sites. If you have the vaguest inkling that a site won't be useful to you, continue onward, or you'll never find your pot of occupational gold. But, however you do use these sites, do not give up hope; with all that information out there, you are bound to find some links and some leads that are perfect for you.

The best place to start your online job-search is at Peter D. Weddle's site. Weddle is the acknowledged master of online resources.

**Weddle's Web Guide**
**www.nbew.com/weddle.html**

If you're going to surf online resources, here's the roadmap. Weddle has compiled information on all types of resources, a sort of directory of directories, and this is the best jumping-off point for your online job-search surfing. Bookmark Weddle's first, then *happy surfing!*

## Career and Job-Search Information Sites

These sites provide general information about the job-search process, résumé writing, relocating, interviewing, getting in touch with recruiters, and related topics. If they have job-search capabilities, they are tangential to these informational features. Use these sites as resources to help you figure out what career direction you would like to take and how to go about the job-search process.

*America's Career Info Net*　　　　　　　　　　　　**www.acinet.org**

This site contains a wealth of information on the job-searching process and on individual careers. You can look up an occupation by keyword and get a general description of the work one does in that field and an occupational forecast. While the site is merely informational, it is linked to all the state employment department home pages, nationwide.

*Career Magazine*　　　　　　　　　　　　　**www.careermag.com**

Browse lists of job fairs, a career consultant directory, and relocation resources. Special to this site is all the information it has on recruiters and career consultants. There are many links to other career-oriented sites and to large employers.

*The Career Builder Network*　　　　　　　　　　**www.careerbuilder.com**

Gives a wealth of information on résumé writing, employer negotiations, interviews, cover letters, and books about the job-search process. Despite existing job listings, the site is best for its informational resources.

*Career and Resume Management for the Twenty-first Century*　　　**www.crm21.com**

Basically an ad board for résumé-writing professionals. Go here if you need résumé assistance and haven't been sure where to find it.

*Catapult on JOBWEB*　　　　　　　　　　**www.jobweb.org/catapult**

This site is a very good information and resource link site, intended for students and recent graduates. There are many topics to choose from to help your career get catapulted into motion.

*Computerwork.com*　　　　　　　　　　　**www.computerwork.com**

Not a place with job listings; contains information on the job-search process and careers in the computer field. A good place for the computer nerd to get a solid grounding before doing an actual job search.

*Internet Career Connection*　　　　　　　　**www.onlinecareerguide.com**

Link central. There are links provided to sites offering job searches, places to post your résumé, résumé services, and guides to getting jobs.

## General Sites for Performing a Job Search and Posting Your Résumé

*4work.com*                                                    **www.4work.com**

This site has a full range of employment opportunities, including job listings for both full-time and part-time work and, most distinctly, listings for volunteer opportunities and internship positions.

*America's Employers*                          **www.americasemployers.com**

Unique for the fact that it has networking chat rooms and allows for real-time, private Internet interviews with reps from hiring companies. Must register (for free) to use these services by submitting your résumé. Otherwise, a good site.

*America's Job Bank*                                       **www.ajb.dni.us**

An excellent site: straightforward and easy to use. It provides salary quotes with job listings and produces a very broad list of openings, despite the specificity of search variables. There are a few pages with job market information, and you can receive help creating an online résumé.

*Best Jobs U.S.A.*                                      **www.bestjobsusa.com**

Provides a career guide, industry news, corporate profiles, and newsgroups to subscribe to. Job search by state, job category, and keyword.

*The Black-Collegian Online*                  **www.black-collegian.com/jobs**

Similar to other general job-search sites, but geared to the African-American college student. Post your résumé, look through a large number of job listings, read about African-American issues in the career world, and explore the online bookstore.

*Blackworld Career Center*                  **www.blackworld.com/careers.htm**

This site provides employment resources for professionals and entrepreneurs from African-American communities in the United States and other ethnic groups worldwide. You can do a job search with very detailed variables or merely by location (either national metros or international gateways).

*Career.Com*                                               **www.career.com**

The best place to search by location; pick a state and you'll get a long and easily browsable list of jobs.

*Career Cast*                                            **www.careercast.com**

Post your résumé or do a basic search. Provides a few good links to career information sources and a list of corporate alliances one can join.

*Career Exchange*                                    **www.careerexchange.com**

An international job-search database and career information center. Includes a conference room to discuss career-related topics with others. View an index of those companies hiring and link to their sites.

*Career Link U.S.A.* **www.careerlinkusa.com**

A "no frills" site; post and search. Job-search variables include a ton of locations and job categories to choose from.

*Career Mosaic* **www.careermosaic.com**

Post your résumé in this site's substantial database. Search for jobs nationally and internationally and view an extensive list of job fairs. See their "College Connection" page for a list of large companies looking for college grads, as well as a list of post-grad internships. There are links to other good career-oriented sites.

*Career Path* **www.careerpath.com**

This site is a database of job openings listed in major Sunday newspapers around the country, job postings from leading employers' Web sites, and job fairs one can attend. Registration is required but is free.

*Career Shop* **www.careershop.com**

Post your résumé for 120 days and search for a job. Review and register for general career training and certification seminars listed here.

*Career Site* **www.careersite.com**

Hook up here with a "virtual agent" who will connect you with employers according to the information you have given in the free registration process. Check each day for your cyberagent's results.

*Career Web* **www.careerweb.com**

Post your résumé or search for a job. Provide your career interest and desired salary information, and the site will then notify you of job listings by e-mail. Despite narrow search variables, searches produce good listing results.

*Classifieds 2000-Employment* **www.classifieds2000.com**

This site has developed partnerships with more than 130 Web sites. Visitors can search more than 100,000 employment listings culled from the 130-plus sites. Pick from such listings in the areas of general job opportunities, featured ("hot") employers, jobs with "cutting-edge start-up companies," and "domestic" jobs. Post your résumé and get a virtual agent to e-mail you with new, matching job listings.

*Connect to Jobs* **www.cabrillo.cc.ca.us/affiliate/connect/index.html**

An excellent database with a California focus—lots of information on electronic job searching and lists of "job boards" (sites with job listings) that are categorized federally, statewide, by career field, etc. Intended for students and counselors; easy to use, lots of information.

*Contract Employment Connection @ NTES* **www.ntes.com**

Intended to link contract professionals with employment opportunities in the temporary/contract job market. You can download all the job listings at this site and peruse them at your convenience. Link to and view recruiter home pages for jobs that may not be at this site.

*e-span* **www.espan.com**

Perform a job search by category, location, and keyword; do an employer search by picking up to five states and five industries, and you'll receive a list of who is actively searching for employees. Post your résumé using their "résumé builder." When you register (no fee), they will e-mail you with new job openings matching your specifications.

*Employment Opportunities and Resume Postings* **galaxy.einet.net/GJ/employment.html**

This is another database of job-listing sites, however these here are far more esoteric. Many links are to the job listing pages of academic institutions, as well as to a number of sites listing federal jobs. It's worth checking out, even though most of the sites are gopher connections and take a few moments longer to hook up.

*Hot Jobs* **www.hotjobs.com**

Offers jobseekers a résumé database with e-mail connections to the member companies in the Fortune 500. There are a good number of variables with which to compose your search and good results are generally produced.

*Inter-Links* **http://alabanza.com/kabacoff/Inter-Links/employment.html**

A great database of the biggest and best job-search Web sites. Includes an excellent section for those looking for jobs in the academic field.

*Job Bank USA* **www.jobbankusa.com**

Connection to a "JobMetaSearch" page, which accesses the Internet's largest employment databases. There are an incredible number of links provided here. Also, search for a job, submit a résumé, and use that "Job Scout" (e-mail agent) to hunt down a job for you.

*Job Center* **www.jobcenter.com**

A very basic site: post a résumé, search for a job. Pay $5 and you can be notified by e-mail of matching employers.

*Job-Hunt* **www.job-hunt.org**

Provides a large number of job listings in varied fields and provides an incredible number of useful links to choose from that will hook you up with general career information and sites with job-search databases.

*Job-Hunt: Science, Engineering, & Medicine* **www.job-hunt.org/sciences.html**

A part of the main **Job-Hunt** site, this page must be noted for the tremendous list of links it provides to other sites where you can find job listings in the various sciences—which seems like a rarity in cyberspace.

*Job Search Sites on the World Wide Web* **www.cco.purdue.edu/Student/jobsites.htm**

The mega-database of job-search databases, a highly recommended site. Provides a comprehensive yet highly categorized grouping of lists of various databases to help you with your job search. An efficient way to narrow down the sites you want to use for job searching. Incredible!

*JobSmart: California Job-Search Guide* **www.jobsmart.org**

Offers job listings in California only. Contains good general career information on résumé writing, career guides, resources for networking in the "hidden job market," many links to sites focusing on Sacramento, San Francisco, Los Angeles, and San Diego. JobSmart has over 200 links to online salary surveys, the largest such collection on the Web. Highly recommended.

*Job Trak* **www.jobtrak.com**

This site is for college students and alumni only. You must first register by picking the campus you're from. Then you can do a job search and receive job-searching tips. Employers pay to post their job offerings; however, it is free to students.

*The Monster Board* **www.monster.com**

One of the oldest, largest, and most active career sites on the Web. Search for a job, post a résumé, visit a topical chat room, link to employers or recruiters, learn about job search, résumé writing, cover letters, "ask the expert," it's all here. From college student to retiree, The Monster Board has something for you. Highly recommended.

*NationJob Network* **www.nationjob.com**

"P. J. Scout" will scout out a job for you and e-mail you on an ongoing basis when something comes up. Also, there is job searching by actual community, as opposed to city or state, and a directory of all companies posting at this site.

*National Business Employment Weekly* **www.nbew.com**

The home page of this site is largely informational, assisting you with job-search strategy, networking, interviewing, and shaping up your résumé. However, it does somewhat fervently point you in the direction of its link to the *Wall Street Journal* page, which provides job listings. Additionally, this is the home of "Weddle's Web Guide," which provides a list of top job-search sites with detailed statistics about each site (number of résumés, top three career areas posted, résumé posting period). Highly recommended.

*Net-Temps* **www.net-temps.com**

The best site for finding temporary work; find permanent work as well. Search by nation, state, or city. Post a résumé that stays active for thirty days. You can post to and read their free general classified pages, an oddity for a career site—get a job, buy a couch, and find a date in their personals, all at one site!

*Online Career Center* **www.occ.com**

This site has many ways to job search. Most distinctly, this site has career resources for women and minorities—links to organizations helping these groups obtain jobs or supporting them in their careers. It also has a plethora of links to sites in industries such as engineering, computers, health care, and human resources.

*Recruiting-Links.com* **www.recruiting-links.com**

Compose a search for the type of job you want; the results will provide you with a list of hiring companies and organizations. You can choose to link from this list to *their* sites, where you can then leave your résumé.

*Telecommuting Jobs* **www.tjobs.com**

This site links jobseekers who want to "commute" to work via electronic means with employers who have appropriate job openings. Job opportunities are available for artists, desktop publishers, photographers, salespeople, writers, data-entry folks, engineers, programmers, Web designers, and the like. Look through job listings, post your résumé for a full year, and post a job wanted ad.

*Town Online* **www.townonline.com/working**

This site is originally out of eastern Massachusetts and therefore provides job listings mostly out of the eastern half of the states. Review job listings, company profiles, lists of job fairs, and an index of career-oriented articles.

*The Wall Street Journal* **www.careers.wsj.com**

An excellent and comprehensive site catering to such industries as business, engineering, utilities, banking, government, etc. Do a job search and post a résumé. There are no listings in general science, medicine, or social service areas. All the information about and links to job hunting, career planning, working with recruiters, human resources issues, and salary profiles you would want. The site has an excellent "career bookstore" with the best job-search/career guidance books available. There is also a list of employers actively recruiting new college grads.

*Westech Virtual Job Fair* **www.vjf.com**

A large number of job listings and lots of information on job fairs and résumé writing.

## Your Doors to the Computer and High-Tech Industries

*American Jobs* **www.americanjobs.com**

For high-tech, computer, and engineering fields, this site gives broad, basic lists of jobs, which include the e-mail addresses of the individuals at the hiring companies to contact about the jobs.

*The Computer Job Store* **www.computerjobs.com**

Pick the "store" you want to go to (one store for each state) and then view the jobs available in that store—like a bulletin board of jobs in your local cafe, only in virtual reality.

*ConsultLink* **www.consultlink.com/consultlink**

This is a high-tech matchmaking service, the place for computer consultants and contractors to the high-tech fields to connect with companies looking for their services. If employers have a project, ConsultLink finds the best candidates (you and your programmer friends) and you are matched appropriately.

*DICE* **www.dice.com**

An excellent site for the techie; one of the great features of this site is its coverage of contract and consulting opportunities, including "high tech permanent, contract, and consulting jobs nationwide for programmers, software engineers, systems administrators,

Web developers, hardware engineers, and others." Also: relocation tools, conventions and conferences, and direct links to employers.

*Select JOBS*                                                    **www.selectjobs.com**

To do a job search you pick your search variables (many to choose from) and then you are asked to register by entering your e-mail address. You are later notified of any new jobs matching your specifications. Cut and paste your résumé. Unique to this site is an extensive listing of user groups categorized by location and skill.

*Silicon Valley Technical Employment Agencies*          **www.sease.com/jobs.html**

This is a site intended for experienced technical consultants and contractors. Through here you are able to have your résumé e-mailed to all the employment agencies in Silicon Valley. The idea behind this site is that e-mail is cheaper than snail mail; the guy running the site has compiled a monster list of Silicon Valley agencies to which he so kindly forwards your résumé for review.

*Skill Scan Résumé Center*                                        **www.skillscan.com**

This site stores the posted résumés of computer professionals (yours included) looking for either contract or permanent work on a CD-ROM database for nine months. This CD is distributed weekly to the nation's top high-tech consulting firms, agencies, and corporations.

*SoftMoonlighter.com*                                  **www.softmoonlighter.com**

This is an excellent site—for computer programmers only. Post your qualifications; when a firm is interested you will be notified via e-mail. There is a great database of computer projects needing programmers; search by language, OS/hardware, GUI, Internet language/Web design, industry, database, location, etc.

*Tech Web*                                               **www.techweb.com/careers**

This site is much like an online magazine, with lots of confusing glitz for high-tech professionals. However, there are many search variables with which to compose your job search and many links to sites giving information on the business aspect of the high-tech industry. There is also a link to a downloading site, including free software.

*Web Staff*                                               **www.web-staff.com/jobs**

A site for those interested solely in Web-related careers (designing, programming, managing, etc.). Good for its specialization, but you can search only by location.

## Sites for the Executive or Executive-to-Be

The following cater to the individual who has at least attained an executive position. If that is what you are pursuing, they may be excellent for making on line connections. Check them out, if you match their demographic.

*CIO.COM*                                                    **http://jobs.cio.com**

Contains postings of senior level IT positions—CIO, VP, director level and above only. Gives an excellent list of executive symposiums and forums and provides links to the groups holding these.

*Exec-U-Net*                                                **www.execunet.com**

"Exec-U-Net is an organization that you join to gain excellent information on job search and career management and to connect with others. It is not a search firm or in the outplacement business." A for-pay newsgroup for executives or those looking to be executives. This site may produce some good leads, if one actively participates in the online opportunities. Slightly East Coast-biased.

*Futurestep*                          **www.futurestep.com/cndt12/sign_in/welcome.asp**

A service from Korn/Ferry and the *Wall Street Journal* for management professionals. Once you register (free), your profile will be available to Korn/Ferry recruiters. Each registrant is promised a "Career Feedback" profile detailing salary market value, "the industry and positions for which you are most suited, the company culture with which you are most compatible, and the areas of expertise on which you can build." If you're in middle or upper management and want to get a recruiter's attention, consider this site.

*The Harvard Business School Club of Chicago*                **http://hbs-chicago.org**

While this site is for the most part information and doesn't list jobs, I list it here because it has some great links to executive-oriented sites. It's a very simple set up; just pick a topic and it will provide you with the executive career links you need. It also provides information about places to search for a job both on and off line. You can even join the Harvard Business School Club of Chicago from here, although you must be a graduate or present or former member of the Harvard School of Business.

*Kennedy Publications*                                      **www.kennedyinfo.com**

Excellent information on executive search consultants, venture capitalists, outplacement firms, and job-search books specifically for the management- and executive-level jobseeker. Has a search engine for headhunters.

*NETSHARE 2000*                                         **www.netshare.com/index1.html**

This is a for-pay site and confidential service "developed for executives who are actively pursuing a new position or simply managing their careers. . . ." Good site for the individual with a substantial amount of experience.

*Ohio State Business Job Finding*                        **www.cob.ohio-state.edu/~cds**

Provides a list of links to companies offering business-oriented positions and general sites with job listings in the business field. Accessible to the home page level from any online computer, to the listing level only from another university's pathway.

*The Recruiting and Search Report*                          **www.rsronline.com**

Excellent information on executive search consultants, with a direct mail merge service that is extremely inexpensive for the level of assistance offered (select, merge, print, sign your name, fold, insert, label, and forward to you for mailing so you get your local postmark). This site also has info on monthly telephone seminars on executive job-search techniques.

### The Search Bulletin                                www.searchbulletin.com

A networking site offering members exclusive access to the executive hidden job market. Members only, a true networking service (find a lead, pass along a lead). One of the older, larger, and more active executive job sites.

### Society of Career Recruiting and Transition Strategists          www.socratescareers.com

A collection of resources for the executive-managerial-professional job search, including executive search firm data, how to find out what your references are really saying about you, reviews of top "how to" publications for management-level candidates, and counseling and coaching services.

## Sites for Those Interested in the Physical, Life, or Social Sciences

### The Bio Career Center                                www.biocareer.com

A nice, public-service-type site sponsored by the Biotechnology Industry Association and SciWeb—The Life Science Home Page. You can post a résumé, search for job listings, and explore career resources for life sciences, from student-level internships to chief scientist opportunites.

### BioMedNet                                           www.biomednet.com

This site is unique for its international job listings of biomedicine-related jobs, but it appears you can't post your résumé. Join for free, and you can then browse their full-text library or bio and medical publications.

### Bio Online                                          www.bio.com

From their home page, go to their career center, pick from a list of biotechnology companies that are presently hiring, and then review their job listings. You may submit a "résumé" to the site, but only using their fill-in-the-blanks form.

### ECO.ORG                                             www.eco.org

This is an odd site. They will help place you in internships in their 600 offices around the United States, but they do not give listings of general environmental jobs. Maybe a good starting place for the individual looking for an environmental career.

### Educational Placement Service                       www.teacherjobs.com

For those who want to have a career in K–12 education, this is the place to go—the largest teacher placement service in the United States and accredited by the National Association of Teacher Agencies. Search through job listings and post your résumé.

### Medical-Ad-Mart                                     www.medical-admart.com

All of the help wanted ads of various medical-related magazines are brought together here in one place, so you can browse them without having to go through the articles to find them!

*Medhunters* **www.medhunters.com**

Connects health-care professionals with employment opportunities worldwide. You don't *have* to register to browse their job listings, but they ask you to do so by filling out their "job specification" forms. And hey! when you do this, "no résumé is required"! A little limiting.

*MedSearch* **www.medsearch.com**

Anything you would like to know about the career or business aspect of the medical field is here. There are links to job databases of various medical companies and hospitals and to professional medical alliances. It has its own "library," with links to different medical groups and societies. You can do a job search at this site, but it appears you must first pay for full access and it is not specific to the casual browser about the actual fee.

*Medzilla* **www.medzilla.com**

Here you can only job search by keyword, but interesting and varied results are obtained. A simple site for job searching and cut-&-paste posting your résumé.

*Physics Job Announcements* **http://xxx.lanl.gov/announce/jobs**

Physics job announcements by type. An incredibly interesting site; perfect for the post-grad physics geek to plow through.

## Searching for a Federal Job

*USA Jobs* **www.usajobs.opm.gov/a.htm**

Job listings include everything from entry level, clerical, and labor to senior executive positions. List of summer work and trainee positions. Federal employment applications on line.

*Federal Jobs Digest* **www.jobsfed.com**

Post your résumé and search for federal job openings by occupational category. This site's a little slow, but it has lots of job listings.

*Fedworld* **www.fedworld.gov/jobs/jobsearch.html**

Here you can browse jobs by state, international location, and for the summer season. There are links to other government sites that have information about particular projects and specific agencies. The most interesting aspect of this site is the library of in-progress government and government-funded projects and research.

*Jobs in Government* **www.jobsingovernment.com**

A site providing a good job database for those seeking positions in government, education, and the public sector throughout the United States and Canada.

*Library of Congress Employment* **gopher://marvel.loc.gov/11/employee/employ**

What an interesting place to work despite government bureaucracy! Here are their current listings.

## Help Us Keep This Link Listing Current

Send your links, suggestions, and comments to **donasher@ix.netcom.com**.

## CHAPTER 15

# How to Get Interviews and Plan and Manage a Job Search

A job search is like a game of chess: It has an opening, middle, and an endgame. You use different strategies in each stage, and you watch every moment for an unexpected opportunity to seize and exploit.

First, you must build a strong opening position, creating a network from which the launch multiple attacks on your objective. In the middle, you must keep track of a large volume of possibilities; an error at this point could turn the tide of the game against you. In the endgame, you must sustain your advantage, close in on your target, and win.

First you must make a personal decision to plan and manage your job search aggressively. Decide to commit resources to your job search, especially *time* and *money*. Make sure you have the raw ingredients: the right mailing address; an answering machine; an e-mail provider; a computer, a typewriter, or access to a computer rental station; plenty of résumés, stationery, second sheets, envelopes, stamps, paper, five-by-eight cards, and an inexpensive postal scale; an appointment book; and a decent place to work. Yes, it is true that you can get a job without any of these things, but it's a heck of a lot easier *with* them.

Even if you decide to use your kitchen table as the "command center" for your job search, you must have access to it; it should be clean and well organized, and the project should not have to compete for your attention with jelly drippings or proximate TVs.

Also, as you begin to get interviews, you will need to have a perfect personal appearance. That means at least one complete outfit, from topcoat to umbrella. Now *is* the time to splurge and buy a new suit of clothes. Pay attention to details and accessories. Do your watch and your shoes fit with your job objective? Do your clothes fit you as you are today? If money is a real problem, borrow the items you need to complete the outfit. You can buy your own "career accessories" after your new job improves your cash flow.

Clothes are far more important than you might believe. They really do need to be *perfect*. It is no accident that the word *suit* is a synonym on Wall Street for a junior executive. It is even a good idea to scout the company before your interview to see how people at your level dress, and imitate them.

Do not muddle through this project with halfway measures. The result is your future. Look good, and you will feel good and be confident.

### Building a Lead List

Your first task is to build a lead list. There are five main sources for job leads:

➤ Networking

➤ Cold contacts

➤ Internet

➤ Headhunters and agencies

➤ Newspapers

Build as big a lead list as you can. Be open-minded. This is your opening game, and you do not want to concede resources before you even assess their potential value. Each of these sources of job leads is critical in its own way. Don't conduct a full-scale job search without developing and exploiting job leads from all five sources.

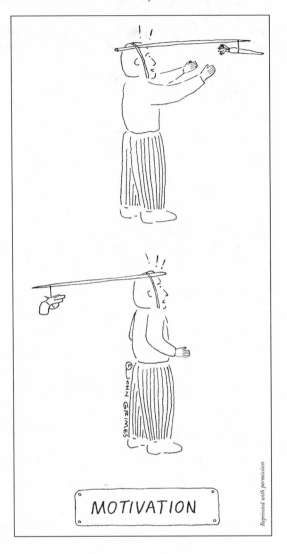

MOTIVATION

*Reprinted with permission*

### Networking

**Networking** is easy. Your targets are everybody you could call on the phone by name. That includes *at least* everyone in your family, all your neighbors, all your friends current and past, all the members of every club or organization to which you belong, every employer or fellow employee of every company at which you have ever worked, all the suppliers and clients with whom you have worked, and every college peer or professor you ever had, and *all their friends and acquaintances.*

This is a pretty big list. For most of us, this is several hundred people, maybe thousands. And it doesn't matter if your contact is as dumb as a post and lives on the other side of the country, either. At all levels, from migrant farm worker to the top echelons of the business elite, some version of personal referral is the number one source of the job lead that results in employment. Here's how you contact the people on your networking lists:

**Hiring Authorities**  **People with the power to give you a job if they want to *whether they are hiring or not.*** They are in the right industry and at the right level to place a hiring order for someone like you.

• You must go **face-to-face** with hiring authorities, if at all possible. Set it up to call them back once every week to ten days *then do it religiously.*

### A Few People or Employers to Contact in Your Job Search

1. Every former employer
2. Every branch, subsidiary, parent, and affiliate of every former employer
3. Every former co-worker
4. Every competitor to every former employer
5. Every supplier or vendor to every former employer
6. Every customer or client of every former employer
7. Every venture or business partner to every former employer
8. Every famous person in your targeted industry, however unlikely your chances of reaching them
9. Every writer at every newspaper or journal that covers your targeted field
10. Every friend you ever had
11. Every friend your friends ever had
12. Every spouse your friends ever had
13. Every parent or close relative your friends ever had
14. Every acquaintance, however fleeting, you ever had
15. Every parent, grandparent, sibling, child, aunt, uncle, niece, cousin, or suchlike you ever had
16. Every friend your parent, etc., ever had
17. Every employer or business associate of any kind your parent, etc., ever had
18. Ever alumnus/alumna of every college or school you ever attended
19. Every professor or teacher you ever had *or who ever worked at* any school you ever attended
20. Every career center officer and career counselor at every school you ever attended
21. Every teacher or professor your kids, siblings, friends, parents, or other relatives ever had
22. Every leader and member of every church, temple, synagogue, ashram, or coven you ever belonged to
23. Every leader and member of every social or academic club you ever belonged to
24. Every leader and member of every professional association you ever belonged to
25. Every neighbor you ever had
26. Every doctor you ever had
27. Every dentist you ever had
28. Every attorney you ever had
29. Every insurance agent you ever had
30. Every dry cleaner or laundry professional you ever had
31. Every stockbroker and financial advisor you ever had
32. Every accountant you ever had
33. Every hairdresser your ever had
34. Every masseuse or masseur you ever had
35. Every personal trainer you ever had
36. Every coach and member of every sports team you ever belonged to
37. Every gym manager or membership director you ever met
38. Every real estate broker you ever had
39. Every auto mechanic you ever had
40. Every veterinarian you ever had
41. Every matchmaker you ever had
42. Every wedding planner or photographer you ever had
43. Every funeral director anyone in your circle of family and friends has ever met
44. Every doorman or doorwoman in every building in the financial district
45. Every clerk in every corner store in your neighborhood
46. Every cabdriver of every cab you ride while your job search is active
47. Every bartender at every club you shouldn't be hanging out in anyway
48. Every psychic you ever consulted, or thought you consulted
49. Every drill sergeant or fellow soldier or sailor you ever served with
50. Start over and talk to them all *again*

**Centers of Influence**  People who, because of their jobs or personalities, come into contact with a very high number of hiring authorities *whether they can help you the first time you call or not.* These are salespeople, consultants, suppliers, journalists, teachers, gossips, and career professionals with a particular industry expertise.

- You must contact these people by telephone every week to ten days *without fail—as if your next job depended on it—*looking for leads, referrals, tips, and gossip about potential employers. Give them copies of your résumé to distribute to others.

**Field or Company Contacts**  People who work in the field or specific companies that you have targeted, *whether they can help you the first time you call or not.* These are all types of workers, from senior executives to janitors. Be sure to consider contacts at suppliers/vendors, customers/clients, competitors, and typical venture partners for the type of company you have targeted.

- You must contact these people by telephone every week to ten days *without fail,* looking for leads, referrals, tips, and gossip about potential employers. Give them copies of your résumé to distribute to others.

**Everybody Else in the World**  Everybody means everybody, *including people you think could have no possible connection to your job search.*

- You must contact these people once with a networking letter (and a copy of your résumé), asking them to call you if they have any tips or leads for you *regarding specific industries, companies, or positions.*

## Cold Contacts

Next, make a list of companies that you would like to **cold contact**. Do not make a fanciful wish list of companies you know nothing about. A good way to start is to make a list of your current employer's vendors, clients, and competitors. Do not forget that the majority of new jobs (entry- to executive-level) are created in small- to medium-sized businesses, not Fortune 500 companies.

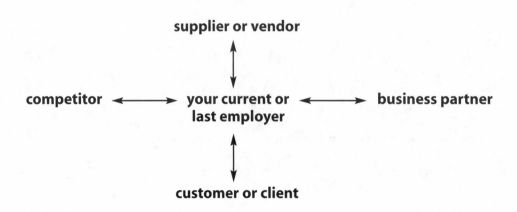

supplier or vendor

competitor ← → your current or last employer ← → business partner

customer or client

Also, before you give up on your current employer, be sure to look for an attractive assignment in other branches, divisions, and cities. Changing employers is expensive and taxing, and you might be able to find exactly what you want somewhere in the far-flung reaches of your own organization.

If your list of companies is short, you can always walk into the business branch of your local library and ask the **reference librarian** for help. There are association directories, industry directories, compilations of local employers by size and industry—all types of data available. Every listing will be a trifle dated, however, and you should verify everything from the corporate headquarters address to whether they have gone chapter seven since the last update. (See appendix, "Annotated Bibliography of Career Books," for more ideas on the vast amount of information out there in reference materials.)

If you live in a major metropolitan area, there are several publishers producing **regional guides,** how-to-get-a-job books complete with company listings, names of key personnel, and similar data. Walk into any major bookstore and ask for a book like this for your region. Remember, every piece of data you read will need to be verified before you can use it. They are mostly useful to give you a place to start if you are new to an area, but don't rely on these books over good old-fashioned research of your own.

Another good source of job leads is the **business press.** If you do not read the trade press for your industry, call them tomorrow morning and subscribe. The articles not only provide you with companies, but with truly important information such as line managers' names, titles, and current pet projects. In any case, you want to be able to talk intelligently about your industry, and reading the trade press is a must.

Needless to say, these lists of companies will overlap your lists of networking contacts. That is, some of your contacts will work at these companies. That is fine. You will launch multiple attacks on these targeted companies anyway.

### Internet

Use the **Internet** to find out about companies in three ways. First, post your résumé on Web sites that database jobseekers. Second, actively seek out companies' "want ads" on Web sites that compile open job listings. Third, and this should comprise the bulk of your effort, seek out companies' own Web sites and submit your résumé in response to their open job listings and their method for accepting electronic résumés. The rule here is *follow the rules.* See chapter 13, "Scannable, Internet, and HTML Electronic Résumés," and chapter 14, "Directory of Career-Oriented and Job-Search Web Sites," for how to get maximum use out of the Internet in your job search, how to use search engines to discover companies, find their home pages, and ferret out their online application process.

Companies like online searches because they can manage a very large amount of client data with very few management hours. Candidates like Internet job searching because e-mail serves as the medium for contact, and they generally don't have to call people. Nobody, however, not even the geekiest techie, should rely only on Internet job leads. Competition here is fierce, statistically, and I've noticed that some people get lots of hits but no jobs. This is a direct result of the fact that they can hide behind the Internet and not develop their job-search communications skills and real-time job-market savvy that only comes from interviewing live, in person, in a suit, and in someone's office.

## Headhunters and Agencies

**Headhunters, employment agencies, college placement offices,** and your **state employment development department** are more sources of job leads. The preceding list is roughly in order of the level of job they represent. The higher up the business ladder you are, the higher up the list you should look. Everyone should contact his or her college placement office once in a while, but state agencies can be full of out-of-date listings for nightmare jobs. This is changing now, however, as state agencies are going fully online with listing and matching services. The master list for all state agencies is listed in the last chapter, www.acinet.org.

There are many books written on headhunters. If you know the headhunters who specialize in your industry, you definitely should use them. If you are currently employed *and* you are making more than $60,000 per year *and* your career has shown rapid advancement in the last five years, then you definitely should contact them. Otherwise, they may not be a good source for you. They still could be, but the odds get considerably slimmer.

Headhunters broker a *lot* of jobs between $35,000 and $60,000, but they work more like agencies to do it. The old maxim was "Agencies find jobs for people; headhunters find people for jobs." In practice, though, the line between employment agencies and executive recruiters has all but disappeared in most states. If your salary falls between $35,000 and $60,000, you could find yourself working with both. Do not expect a lot of frills and hand holding in this range.

I would definitely recommend that you avoid any organization that wants you to pay a fee, but otherwise, depending on your level, you should make some targeted contacts in agencies or recruiting firms. Warning: If you want to switch careers, placement specialists are not going to be too excited about speaking with you.

You can look in the Yellow Pages under "Executive Search Consultants" for headhunters and under "Employment Agencies" for agencies. A better trick is to call the directors of human resources for major companies in your industry and ask them what headhunters they use. Of course, while you are asking, you may as well ask for an informational interview at the same time.

If you are a solid executive-level candidate, call Kennedy Publications at (603) 585-6544 and ask for *The Directory of Executive Recruiters*. This book is rarely available in bookstores. This directory is a little complex, but you will be able to sort executive recruiters by industry, function, and location. They also have a free Web site with a recruiter search engine and online career bookstore: www.kennedyinfo.com. The Recruiting and Search Report publishing company also provides headhunter data for a very reasonable fee; call (800) 634-4548 or (904) 235-3733.

I will tell you what to do with the list later, but try to target agencies and recruiters that work with people like yourself.

## Newspapers

If you are at the management level, check the **newspaper** only once a week, on Sunday for most metropolitan papers, although Monday is also a big career day in some markets. Tuesday is the conventional day for listing new management positions in the *Wall Street Journal.* You may wish to subscribe to the *WSJ*'s *National Business Employment*

*Weekly,* a compilation of the job ads in all four regional editions of the *WSJ* combined with topical articles on job searching at the management level. Call (800) JOB HUNT, or (609) 520-7314 to subscribe.

If you are a lower-level candidate, check the papers every day. Caution: No one should use the papers as the sole source of job leads. Be sure to use the other sources discussed above as well.

The newspaper is a good place to get ideas and to get a feel for the job market in your field. Also check industry and trade publications, which usually have some kind of career want ads section. Advertisements have a bad reputation as a source of job leads, the result of two unrelated facts: First, many of the most important career books in the last decade were written by headhunters, and, second, advertisements generate considerable competition for you, the candidate.

Headhunters have a vested interest in coming between you and the in-house recruiters at companies. Obviously, this prejudice does not concern you.

If you have followed the straightforward instructions in this book, your résumé will win against heavy competition. If you are a good candidate with a good résumé, you have little to fear.

Remember, however, that study after study has shown that more than **70 percent of all jobs change hands in the hidden job market,** and that means networking and direct contact to companies *before* they run any kind of advertisement.

Build as large a lead list as you can. Benchmark: **You need 100 active leads at all times during your job search.** If you don't have 100 leads, you can't look for a job systematically. You might find one by accident, but that's what it will be: an accident.

## The Telephone Is Your Best Friend

To paraphrase the late Mayor Daley, call early and call often. Call all your networking contacts and alert them to your job search. Tell them what you are looking for, and ask them if they have any ideas. Ask them to keep an ear out for any leads and be sure to tell them you will be calling them back next week. Then do it. It is also a good idea to send them a copy of your résumé with a short note, reminding them of your call. Give them permission to forward the résumé to interested parties. (Remember, this plan is for a full-scale job search. If you are employed, you may wish to think twice before spreading your résumé from coast to coast.)

**Do not ask your contacts for a job; ask for ideas and referrals.** This is called lowering the ante. Likewise, when you begin to contact employers, ask for ideas, introductions to third parties, information, informal interviews, brief meetings, conversations, anything but a job. Asking for a job puts them on the spot. When you lower the ante, your contact is genuinely relieved, and that relief translates into a greater willingness to help you with a meeting or a viable job lead.

If a targeted employer says they are not hiring, you have two options. Ask to interview anyway. Say something like, "Even if you don't need anyone now, I'd like you to know what I have to offer. Then if something opens up, you'll think of me first." Or, you can ask for an informational interview about the position that is not open and the company and industry in general. Use this type of contact to gain intelligence about the type of position you are interested in and to get referrals to other companies or divisions or departments where you might be needed now. The fact that a company is not hiring has no bearing on its potential value to your job search.

— —

**Five Questions to *Always* Ask in Informational Interviewing**

1. **How did *you* get into this?**

2. **What educational or experiential preparation is typical to get into this? Of what is typical, what, if any, is *required*?**

3. **What was different from what you expected? What was the biggest surprise when you went into this? Any myths you want to shatter for me?**

4. **What advice do you have for someone like me?**

5. **Who else does this? What other companies? Who else should I be talking to?**

And maybe a sixth question could be about career paths: "Where does this go?" "What does this prepare you for next?" "What's next for you?" or "What ensures *continued* success in this field?" And maybe a seventh question could be about salary. If you ask about salary, don't ask about *their* salary or even salaries at *their* companies. Ask: "What could a person expect to make in a position like this?" or "What would be a typical salary industry-wide for a position like this?" Then subtract 10 to 40 percent.

— —

## Call → Write → Call

Whether you have a lead on an opening or a lead that could lead to a lead on an opening, you approach all contacts roughly the same way: Call and get the exact name, title, and mailing address of your key contact. Find out if she is in town at this time. Try to get a little information on the opening, if there is one. Do this in every case except when responding to a newspaper ad that demands "no calls." If you can find a network lead into a company with a "no calls" ad, by all means, call, cite your network connection, and proceed as though you had never seen their ad. Do not hesitate to approach a company at multiple levels and through multiple channels, especially large companies. I have had clients receive routine rejection slips from companies long after they started to work there.

Then, send in your résumé and cover letter addressed to your contact. Be sure to say in your letter that you will be calling, and *specify what day you will call*. Here is a great line:

> I will call you on Tuesday before noon. You can count on me to be prompt. I look forward to our conversation.

Schedule your follow-up call no later than the close of the next business day after they get your letter. This is critical. If you don't call right away, your materials will have disappeared into the system. Obviously, you will need to estimate when they will get the letter, so consider a reliable method. The simplest way to start is to ask if she got your letter. If not, great, you have an excuse to call again. Say who you are, tell her you will send her another one, then call back again.

Use these calls as an opportunity to inquire about their hiring process. I am an advocate of total honesty. If someone asks you who you are and what you want, tell her in as honest and forthright a manner as possible. You will be surprised at her willingness to help you. Ask what the most important criteria for the position are, find out who is making the decision and how her interview cycle works, ask everything you need to know to be a good candidate. Be sensitive to their needs. Always ask, "Is this a good time to ask a quick question, or would you rather I call back?" Right when a company first opens in the morning is the best time to call. Call before the company even opens, and you can often reach a top officer working early.

If I were launching a job search myself, I would not bother to send a letter or a résumé to anyone without calling first and without calling to follow up. Then, unless you decide you do not want the job, *ask for an interview.* Do not wait for them to decide to interview you, ask for an interview! Remember to lower the ante. Say something like, "That sounds very interesting. Do you think I could stop by to talk about it, at your convenience of course?"

If this sounds simple, it is. This is it. This is how you get interviews. You call and ask for them.

The telephone is your best friend. Use it.

According to Richard Bolles in *What Color is Your Parachute,* it takes 1470 mailed résumés to get a job, but according to research we've done in my office, it takes only fifteen phone calls to get an interview.

If you're not getting enough action in your search, call up **networking** contacts and ask them if they would have just a moment to share advice, ideas, leads, and referrals with you, and call up **targeted companies** and just blatantly ask if they will interview you. They'll have the following objections:

1. **They say, "I'm too busy."**
   *You say,*
   - (a) "This will only take a moment."
   - (b) "I'd be happy to meet you anytime you like, before or after work or even at lunchtime. This'll only take a moment."
   - (c) "Sounds like you need some help down there."

2. **They say, "We're not hiring."**
   *You say,*
   - (a) "That's okay. I'm not looking for a job with you anyway. I just wanted to know if you had a moment to share with me any advice, ideas, leads, or referrals."
   - (b) "That's okay. I'm not in any hurry. I heard you're a great place to work, and I just wanted to know if you had a moment to meet with me in case something opens up later."

3. **They say, "I'm not the person you should talk to."**
   *You say,*
   - (a) "Great. I'd be happy to follow your normal procedures. Who is it I should be contacting?"
   - (b) "Well, I'm also pursuing contacts through your 'official' channels, but I just wondered if you had a moment to share any advice with me."

**4. They say, "Send me your résumé and I'll think about it."**
*You say,*

   (a) "Let me fax it to you, and I'll call you right back. What's your fax number?"

   (b) "Let me tell you what's on it. Here's a brief synopsis. . . ."

Be consistently nice; cite any referrals, mutual acquaintances, or connections; and just keep trying. Focus on getting advice and referrals, and you'll get a lot further than if you focus only on known openings. Get there before the opening is announced!

Look carefully at the above scripts, and you will realize that you could call anybody, at random, in a targeted company and ask if he had any advice for you on how to get hired.

Your calls will not work every time, of course, but every time you call you will be closer to your next job.

Remember, **if you're always in the right place, sooner or later it's the right time.**

In one of the worst recessions in automotive history, we stuck a new college graduate in a closet in Flint, Michigan, with a phone and the above scripts. We told him to call automotive-related companies and ask them if they had just a moment to look at his résumé and give him advice. At the end of the first day, he had eight interviews scheduled. At the end of the week, he had a job. Much more experienced engineers stayed unemployed for months, and some for years, while our young novice went to work and earned a paycheck.

Nothing is better and nothing is faster than calling employers on the phone.

## Job Search Protocol, Momentum, and Timing

One of the most important aspects of a job search is momentum. I once worked with a very talented CFO who blew lead after lead by failing to follow up in a timely manner. He thought a week was fast enough to get out a follow-up letter. He thought three to four days was fast enough to return a call. Time after time, I saw the hiring authority's excitement fade away before my candidate made his next move.

Timeliness is next to godliness. You must call by the close of the next business day after your material lands on the desk of your target. After that, your application, letter, or idea is dead meat. Nobody can find it, nobody knows anything about it, and nobody cares. So be prompt, create urgency, demonstrate how "on top of it" you are.

Obviously, you need some way to tell when your mailing will arrive. The U.S. mail has become the dumping ground for second- and third-class junk. Even first-class mail between two buildings in the financial district can be totally unreliable, with delivery varying between one to four days. And you have to allow some time for the company's internal mail distribution system, another variable.

Consider alternate delivery. Within a city you can send your résumé by messenger. These ubiquitous carrier pigeons can penetrate well into companies, placing your envelope right on the desk of the person you seek. Write directly on your nine-by-twelve envelope, "URGENT-via MESSENGER." Then call the next morning. If you are applying to another city, use an overnight courier service. Then call the morning after it arrives.

If the company provides a fax number for applicants, *always* use it. They may be in a hurry to interview applicants. However, if you fax you résumé or submit via e-mail, then go ahead and mail a copy in also. You're looking for a job, not Brownie points.

Although the following points are probably overwhelmingly obvious to you, I have been surprised that many people do not know them:

➤ Never, never, never send a résumé without a cover letter, or a fax without a cover sheet. The best thing that can happen is it will get lost before it can damage your reputation.

➤ Never use stationery, envelopes, or the postage meter from your current employer. It smacks of disloyalty, and is, in fact, theft. However, feel free to use your business cards.

➤ Never put any comment about salary requirements in a cover letter. You will disqualify yourself automatically from jobs you might enjoy. Many employers can be convinced to pay far more than they planned if they like you, but they are not going to like you very much if you do not give them a chance. This is a quintessential example of a throw-out factor. Ironically, you may even disqualify yourself from a higher salary for the job you eventually accept. If you do feel compelled to comment on salary, speak in vague ranges, not exact figures. Still, it is better to reveal this information later. Remember, you are not supposed to be sending your résumé to anyone you do not plan to call.

**"Occasionally I like to answer the phone in person . . . it really freaks them out!"**

➤ Always show up for meetings five minutes early. If you are held up at one interview, call the next one and reschedule it for the next available time, rather than going in late. If you are unemployed, be careful that your internal clock does not get "loose." I worked with a displaced vice president of a major bank. Early in the search he showed up five minutes early for everything, but as the project wore on, he began to act as though 9:08 were the same thing as 8:55. **It is not.**

➤ Never say anything bad about a former employer. If you are very angry at a former employer, only practice will allow you to say nice things about him. Practice with your spouse, your dog, your rearview mirror. Say only nice things, out loud. You really do have to do these rehearsals; otherwise, you will blow opening night. At the top levels of management, a candidate can explain, dispassionately, where an employer may have made a strategic error, but otherwise, follow the rule.

➤ Avoid any attitude that can be interpreted as "I don't know how you can get by without me." This is evident in such common statements as, "I know I will be an invaluable asset to your organization," or "I know I could solve that $54 million marketing problem for you within six months." Employers find this attitude presumptuous and offensive. Of course you want these things to be true, but to say them outright is a mistake.

Instead, find out how you actually would fit into the organization and discuss how your skills would be applied. If there is a fit, both you and your potential employer will know it.

If you are not at the management level and your job skills are readily available in a large number of other candidates, then timeliness can be everything. In some markets you can buy the Sunday paper on Friday or Saturday. Get your letters in the mail by Saturday night, and they will start arriving Monday morning. Your potential employer will be impressed and may even wonder how you could respond to an ad in the Sunday paper on the Saturday before.

Better yet, hand deliver your résumé the moment the company opens on Monday. Do not be pushy in asking for an impromptu interview, as many business people view unnecessary interruptions about the same way a horse views a snake.

If youth, vitality, and eagerness are your main job qualifications, you cannot apply too early, follow up too exactly, or be too polite. Do not succumb to the temptation to concoct a "creative" résumé; every employer has a drawer full of these things, all from people she has never interviewed.

Make a straightforward, skills-based résumé. If you want to be creative, use an unorthodox delivery system. Everybody knows the story about the scriptwriter who threw his opus over the producer's pool fence. I would not bother people at home, but have you considered rolling your résumé up, tying it with a silver ribbon, tossing it in a mailing tube so it has a nice rattle, marking it "URGENT," and sending it via messenger?

Of course, none of these tricks will work unless you pick up the phone and follow up with a call.

Here is one of my favorite lines, which can be used to give the impression that you have not been looking for a position at all: "One of my friends alerted me to your recent advertisement." With this line, you can respond to ads weeks late. Be prepared to name the friend in the interview.

The hiring cycle at some companies is longer than you could imagine. Even if they have placed someone in the position, sometimes that person does not work out, and your application arrives just as that becomes apparent. Or the person they hired may hire *you*, as she rebuilds the management team. Be open to these possibilities and view newspaper ads as just another way to get into a company. Once you are inside, you can look in all directions for the right fit.

Always call one day in advance to confirm your appointments. It is also a good idea to discuss the objectives of the meeting. I had a client who was a whizbang at translating computer science and mathematical research papers from German, Dutch, and French into English. He won an interview with the hottest cult company in Silicon Valley at the time. Everybody wanted to work there, and this company was practically begging my client to come down and interview.

He had an appointment with *five* key executives. Five department heads were going to converge and meet with this candidate. Five management staff members were planning to disrupt their schedules for him. His human resources person, the one who had coordinated this affair, the one whose you-know-what was on the line, called him to confirm the meeting. Something was wrong with his tape machine, so he never got the message. And he never called. He showed up five minutes early all right, but it was too late. The atmosphere was hostile, the meeting did not go smoothly, and they decided they had better find themselves another whizbang.

After every interview, do two things:

First, write down what happened, with attention to the interviewer's key concerns. For example, the last person to hold the job may have been dynamite at organization and follow-through but lousy at dealing with irate clients on the phone. So the hiring authority's key motivator may be your customer-service skills. You will need detailed notes to remember these keys as you continue to have a large volume of interviews and contacts.

Then, *that very same day,* write a short, sincere thank-you note and get it into the mail. Your interviewer will be most favorably impressed to receive this promptly. (Messenger or courier service may seem pretentious for this follow-up, so use the mail and hope.) For lower-level positions, a tasteful card may be sufficient; at middle to higher levels, a typed note on monarch-sized stationery is acceptable. If the interview and the company are both informal, you may decide that a *readable* handwritten note will be sufficient. Under no circumstances should you write by hand on a full-sized sheet of paper. You must type a more formal thank-you letter if you use this size of paper.

Another use of a follow-up letter is to address some issue brought up in the interview, or to recoup from some faux pas. If the interviewer thought you lacked direct outside sales experience, this might be a good time to drive home that you were the largest-selling cookie monster the Girl Scouts ever had in the state of Iowa. I think you get the picture.

Needless to say, in any interview you should ask about their hiring process, how many interviews they plan, what the competition is like, and when they plan to make their decision. At the end of the interview, ask, "When will I see you again?" or, "When should I call you back?" Never leave the ball entirely in their court.

Here is a line to get past any employer's don't-call-us-we'll-call-you: "I know you'll be in touch with me, Bob, but when, if I haven't heard from you, should I give *you* a ring?"

Be nice to everybody. Turn every dead end into a new networking lead. Tell them you will check in with them in a week, just in case. Then do it.

It is rare to get a management job in less than three interviews, and up to seven interviews is not uncommon. Job-search protocol has become more important than ever, with executive positions going to the Emily Post crowd over better qualified, but less polished, applicants. You must care about these details and attend to them promptly, or the position will go to someone who does.

## Organizing and Managing the Search Project

Now that you have some understanding of what you will be doing in your job search, you can see that this is a lot of detail to manage. You will have to track and control this large project, with hundreds of potential contacts. You will soon find that John is out of town, Jane cannot come to the phone right now, Peter is not the one you should talk to after all, and so on.

I recommend that you use a simple mechanical tool: five-by-eight cards. I have had clients build contact management databases on their PCs that they can sort by multiple fields and keys, but five-by-eight cards will work just fine. Alphabetize by company or contact name, whichever you remember best, and then sort by *date of next activity*. You can make your notes directly on the card. John will be back on May 23. At 8:55 A.M. on May 23, you will call. Jane's secretary said call back tomorrow. Tomorrow you will be sure to call. And so on. Below is a sample notation card. Remember, you might have *hundreds* of these cards active at once.

---

*PIONEER PLATE GLASS*

*2703 Industrial Way  555-2613*

*contact: Tom Angstadt, Production Engineer, Springfield Plant*

— *called 8/7/00, spoke re positions as cost analyst, referred me to Chris Smythe ♂ in account*

— *called C. Smythe, 8/7/00, out of town til Monday*

— *called C. Smythe, 8/13/00, "not available" left message*

— *called C. Smythe, 8/14/00—"in a meeting" left message*

— *8/14/00, 4:30 PM. called Tom Angstadt back, asked him to call C. Smythe*

— *8/15/00, called C. Smythe @ 9 AM. "not available"*

— *called T. A. back, asked him again, he said he'd do it right then*

— *9:30 C. Smythe called, we spoke of cost analyst position, he said he didn't need one, but send resume anyway. Resume mailed 8/15/00, PM*

— *called C. Smythe 9 AM 8/17/00. got resume. nice conversation. he was interested in my experience in payroll. appt set for next Weds.*

— *8/22/00. met C. Smythe. Good meeting. Met CFO Lawrence Steadsitter. goes by "Larry." toured Springfield plant. Met plant mgr. Charles Johnson—"Chuck" seems to be really informal place*

— *Said he had projects for cost analyst—not full position. Sent follow up letter to Steadsitter, (1) offering to do the projects on contract, & (2) asking to apply for other accounting openings. Sent note to C. Smythe*

— *8/27/00. Called Steadsitter. good talk. set meeting for 3 PM with plant manager and Smythe. Wants to create bridge position, ½ cost analysis, ½ staff accountant*

— *JOB OFFER!! 8/27/00 6 PM*

---

Set **quantified goals** for new applications **each week;** follow-ups do not count. A goal of as few as ten new applications per week will soon snowball into a rolling mass of details and follow-up tasks. You must set an ambitious goal for new applications, or you will soon find yourself busy as heck with nothing really going on. You will think things are going great, but your job search could start to wind down before you get any offers. Set *specific, quantified* goals in advance for new contacts per week, then track and check your performance.

Balance your time between your five sources of contacts: networking, direct contacts, Internet, headhunters and agencies, and the newspapers. Put up to 50 percent of your effort into networking and personal referral, but no more than 25 percent into any other one source.

Take every Friday afternoon off from your job search, but set aside Sunday evening to review the last week and to plan the next one. If you have not met your quota for the week, you can respond to some of the ads in the Sunday paper to meet your quantified target for new applications. If possible, have a friend call or stop by on Sunday night, every Sunday night, to whom you will make a report of your activity. Even better, find two or three people who are also looking for employment and start your own job club.

I once worked with a gentleman leaving the air force who formed such a job club with three of his friends. I wrote his résumé and his three friends copied the style perfectly. They each read one get-a-job book and reported on it to the others. Their searches were as professionally thought out and well managed as any I have ever witnessed. Their group served as a crucible for ideas and a place to share the ups and downs of the job-search process.

## Once You Start to Get Offers

No matter what, do not stop sending out new applications. Meet your quota for new applications right up until the day you start your new job. If you find yourself in the hospital in a full body cast during your job search, I want you to send out *a minimum of ten new contacts per week.*

If you get an offer, make sure it is a firm offer. Ask point blank, "Are you offering me the position?" If so, ask, "On what terms?" If you have a firm offer for the job you want, accept it and get something in writing before you leave. Obviously, this is easier if you have calculated in advance what you consider to be your minimum salary and other terms you would require.

If you have a firm offer and are not positive you want it, it is perfectly within bounds to say you need to sleep on it and you will call them tomorrow. Be sure the offer stands. On more than one occasion I have seen a candidate come back to accept an offer that either had never been formally extended or had been withdrawn because it was not accepted immediately. If you stall more than a few days, many employers will retract the offer, with or without telling you.

If the position is not right for you, decline it. You learned a lot in applying for it, and you can use that experience in your continuing search for a position that *is* right for you.

## Salary Negotiations

The general rule about salary is to bring it up as late in the game as possible. Do not respond to a written request for salary history before you have an interview. Acknowledge the request by noting "Salary: Negotiable" at the bottom of your cover letter, but do not address the issue further. Providing salary data before an interview *can only count against you.*

**SUNDAY NIGHT SCORECARD—THE JOB-SEARCH WEEKLY REPORT**

LIST OF <u>NEW</u> CONTACTS                                             (ten minimum)

1) _____

2) _____

3) _____

4) _____

5) _____

6) _____

7) _____

8) _____

9) _____

10) _____

n) _____


NEW CONTACTS FROM NETWORKING:              _____    _____
(up to 50 percent of total effort)                        number    % of total

NEW CONTACTS FROM COLD-CALLING:            _____    _____
(up to 50 percent of total effort)                        number    % of total

NEW CONTACTS WITH HEADHUNTERS & AGENCIES:  _____    _____
(no more than 25 percent of total effort)                 number    % of total

NEW CONTACTS FROM ADVERTISEMENTS:          _____    _____
(no more than 25 percent of total effort)                 number    % of total

---

**LIST OF FOLLOW-UP ACTIVITIES: (should be more than one page, *at least*)**


**FIRST INTERVIEWS:**


**CALL-BACK INTERVIEWS:**


**OFFERS:**


**GOALS FOR NEXT WEEK:**

In the early stages of your interview process, respond to an inquiry about salary requirements or salary with an inquiry of your own: "What range did you have in mind?" No matter what their response, try to deflect the conversation away from salary and back onto the position or your qualifications. Say something like, "We're in the same ballpark, but I am really more interested in the job and what it entails. Could we come back to this later?"

A similar line is, "Well, that doesn't seem unreasonable, but I really need to know more about the position before I could say exactly what I think would be fair."

Another line is, "That seems a little low for what you are expecting from this position, but let's talk further because I really like the company and the people I've met so far."

Always speak in vague ranges, like "mid to high fifties" or "something close to six figures." Do not disqualify yourself unless you and the potential employer really are in completely different ballparks. Wait until they offer you a position.

Only when you get a "Yes" to your question, "Are you offering me the position?" should you begin to discuss the issue in earnest. Then, quote your total compensation package.

---

### How to Turn $43,000 into $68,800

| | |
|---|---:|
| Your base pay: | $43,000 |
| Plus your estimated bonus: | 4,000 |
| Plus your next raise, if imminent: | 4,300 |
| Plus the value of your perks: | |
|     Company auto that you drive 25,000 miles per year: | 13,000 |
|     Matching contribution to company-sponsored retirement plan: | 2,000 |
|     Life and health insurance: | 1,900 |
|     Average four sick days each year your company lets you cash out: | 600 |
| **Your compensation package:** | **$68,000** |

---

Include your company car, insurance, and other benefits in your quote, but focus their quote on cash. *Know the score.* Do not walk into this meeting wondering how much you make now or how much you will require to accept this position. I recently met with a client who was in tears because she negotiated a new job with a total compensation package *below* the job she was leaving. She concentrated on cash, but forgot to account for huge differences in benefit programs between the two employers.

Do not lose a job because of salary negotiations. If they will not match your cash needs, get the difference in perks, signing bonus, incentive bonus, club fees, extra vacation, generous retirement fund contributions, child care, fancy insurance, moving expenses, a fat expense account, paid education, you name it. Creativity and flexibility here can keep your career moving along. Rigidity can make the employer think you are afraid to take a risk and can result in losing an opportunity that you could have benefited from in the long run.

If a position really contributes to your five-year goals, it is usually a good idea to take it at any salary.

When you finally do accept a position, you are off the market. *No matter what,* you must reject all other offers that come in. Show the same integrity you expect of your employer.

## Do Not Oversell Yourself

My clients are generally fairly aggressive. They are committed to advancing their careers and to performing in the positions they take. I have had clients negotiate pay increases as high as $90,000 just to switch jobs. That's right, *a raise* of $90,000. Salary increases of $20,000 to $30,000 are a matter of routine. However, every one of these clients is fully qualified to perform in these new positions.

My goal in this book, and my goal in life, is to get you the best job for which you are qualified, and nothing more. If you apply for jobs for which you have no qualifications and for which you have not substantiated any material interest and for which you have not prepared yourself, then you will not succeed.

If you use the tricks in this book ruthlessly, you will find yourself in interviews for positions far beyond your capacity to perform. But don't underestimate your interviewers. They usually can weed you out *in seconds.* If you are really interested in a career path, research it. Find people who are excelling in this field now and ask them how they got into it.

Do not abuse the techniques provided in this book. Use them to get the very best job in which you can excel. Nothing more, nothing less.

## Psychology of a Job Search

There is a certain pattern to the emotional life of a jobseeker: He will experience some **identity loss** right away and may reconsider his value as a human being. Americans are particularly bad about over-identifying with their careers. To combat this, focus on your family life and your past successes, and remind yourself that you will have a work life again. Take time to be with your kids. Seek out and rediscover your friendships, which have an emotional as well as practical impact on the success of your job search.

In the first stages of her search, a jobseeker may be overconfident and think that this won't take very long at all. She'll be in **denial** about how long this search might last, how much this process may cost, and what she may have to do that is unpleasant or uncomfortable. She may even feel pretty good about all the new possibilities available.

This lasts until the *first* time the jobseeker doesn't get a job he thinks he should have gotten. He is shocked at the number of other well-qualified candidates, the pickiness and pettiness of employers, the rude behavior of recruiters, and the unfamiliar and sometimes demeaning gyrations the job-search process demands of him. Then the jobseeker gets in touch with his **anger.**

Anger is a normal response, but dwelling in anger is very dangerous. *Anger can double the duration of your job search.* One can get over it by having realistic expectations, by deciding to move on from whatever resentments one may have about the old employer, and by anger- and stress-management techniques such as exercise, well-planned leisure activities, family support, a carefully maintained daily-living routine, and counseling.

Sometimes a jobseeker will pass through a period of **deal making,** when she tries to bargain with powers entirely outside her control. She may say to herself, "If I can just get this next interview, I'll never quit another job in my life!" Deal making is common, but irrational.

Then, if a search proves difficult, expensive, and time-consuming, the jobseeker may go into a period of **depression.** The important thing to remember is that it is perfectly normal to be depressed under these circumstances. But just as with anger, depression carries risk. Depression is energy sapping, and you need your energy. Treat short depression as normal, but any prolonged period of depression should be treated by a professional therapist. Whether you seek outside help or not, be sure to pursue known remedies: physical exercise, relaxation exercise, bright lighting, volunteering, well-planned leisure activities, family support, careful attention to personal grooming, a light and varied diet, and a carefully maintained daily routine.

Of course you may experience these phases in any order, or all at once. Even the most hard-driving type-A manager will experience these psychological impacts of a job search. Hopefully, they will be both brief and mild.

The final stage, emotionally, is a **new norm;** that is, the jobseeker now views her job search as her normal life, in effect, *her new job.* In this stage, she can take satisfaction in doing her job search well. She learns about job-search techniques the same way she'd learn about any new set of tasks required by her job, breaks up her job-search projects into manageable portions, takes satisfaction in completing intermediate goals, and stops torturing herself with blame and anger about her condition.

Know about these psychological stages and anticipate them. Remember to look back at this section when you feel you're the only one going through this difficult time. You're not. It's normal. This too shall pass. The fact is, when this is over, you're most likely to be happier than you were before you left your last job.

*And no matter what, even when you are in the depths of despair, keep sending out new applications.*

I recently learned this Japanese proverb from my friend Patrick Combs, a motivational speaker specializing in career issues: **Fall down seven times. Stand up eight.**

MISTER BOFFO © Joe Martin. Universal Press Syndicate. Reprinted with permission. All rights reserved.

# Cover Letters: Don't Write One Until You Read Chapter 15

## CHAPTER 16

Cover letters serve as routing slips for the résumé. Their primary purpose is to get your résumé in front of a viable contact and to motivate that contact to read further. The more you concentrate on this function, the "routing slip" function, the more successful your cover letters will be.

Cover letters are usually read only once or twice, to route your résumé to the persons who acts on it and to spur that action. That action may be to throw your mailing away, to file it, to set it aside with a stack of others, to set it aside to wait for your call, or to call you right away. Obviously, you want one of the latter possibilities.

Do not put critical information in only your cover letter. All critical and substantive points belong in your résumé, yet another reason the profile résumé is so powerful—your skills and abilities are on the document that counts, not the routing slip.

To control the routing of your résumé you always want to write to a person, not a title, a department, or a company. As explained in the last chapter, you must make your phone calls and get the exact name, title, and address of your contact. If your telephone inquiry is not successful, only then should you resort to writing to a title or department, or *several titles* and *several departments*.

The one exception to the call-first rule is a blond box ad in a newspaper. These ads do not name the advertising company, so you do not know whom to call. If you are employed, you should be especially wary of these ads anyway. If you are unemployed or everyone at your company knows you are seeking new employment, then you really have nothing to lose but the postage. Blind box ads have an undeserved bad reputation. Companies have many good reasons for not announcing their hiring plans, ranging from employee relations to competitive issues.

> **To break into blind box ads, use these techniques:**
>
> 1. Ad has street mailing address, but company is not named: Drive by, use a reverse directory available at your library, or use one of the Internet address and phone research sites.
>
> 2. Ad has a post office box, but company is not named. Walk into the post office and say, "According to USPS communication 352.44 'Disclosure of Names and Addresses of Customers,' paragraph 4, 'Post office box address,' section 1, 'Business use,' you are required to provide me with the name, address, and telephone number of this advertiser." The local postmaster must assist you with this whether the box in question is physically at that station or not.
>
> 3. Ad has a box *in care of* the newspaper, but the company is not named: Bribe the newspaper mailroom staff (just kidding) or profile the company based on whatever information is in the ad. For example, if they say they are a "$10 million rubber recycling plant based in the Midwest seeking a cost-accounting manager," you identify *all* the rubber recycling plants based in the Midwest. Then you call them up one by one and ask for human resources or the CFO, saying, "I heard you were looking for a cost-accounting manager . . ." The worst thing that will happen is you'll find some *other* rubber recycling plant needing a cost-accounting manager.

By the way, any time you don't have enough to do in your job search, sit down and start calling companies at random and say this: "I heard you were looking for a [whatever you are]. Who would I talk to about that?" You'll have interviews by the end of the day.

Your response rate to your mailed applications will drop drastically any time you do not address your cover letter to a particular person. Every company has a standard procedure for processing unsolicited résumés, and it is usually designed to get rid of them. Having your résumé filed for "future consideration" with the human resources department is about as useful has having it sucked into a black hole.

The number-one way to avoid this procedure is to identify your mailing as a "personal" or a "solicited" mailing. In your very first paragraph, cite your telephone call or your personal referral source. Very few clerks are willing to take the risk of sending your material to the black hole if it looks like somebody in the company is expecting it, or you may be somebody important, or know somebody important. If you can't come up with another line, use this one: "Donald Asher recommended that I write directly to you. I'm interest in positions in . . ."

Here are some introductory paragraphs demonstrating this technique:

> Dear Ms. Jacobs:
>
> I was discussing Hyatt operations with Joseph DiMarco, and he suggested that you might be interested in someone with my background. My expertise is IT for hospitality businesses. In the interest of discussing employment opportunities with you, I have enclosed my résumé for your review.

> Dear Ms. Snyder:
>
> We met a few weeks ago in Chicago at the Ritz Carlton while Nick McRobie was giving a demonstration of Acom software packages. Ever since our conversation

about your aggressive projects to retool for the '00s, I have been thinking about discussing employment opportunities with you. Toward that end, I have enclosed my résumé for your review.

Dear Mr. van den Burgh:

I was discussing my job search with Lars Lundgren recently, and he mentioned you quite favorably. He gave me your current address, and suggested that I contact you directly. Since I saw you last . . .

The same technique works with headhunters. If you are a personal referral, your résumé will be handled differently than an unsolicited mailing.

Dear Ms. Taylor:

I got your name from a professional acquaintance, Mr. Dale Shaw, director of human resources for Majorfees Corp. He said you often have clients who would be interested in someone with my background. Accordingly, I am sending my résumé for your review.

If you are applying for a known opening, cite that opening *as part of your heading.* Try not to make anyone actually read your cover letter in order to tell what position you are seeking.

Attn: Ms. Tony Bonetti, Director, Management Recruiting

Re: Company Representative, Asia/Pacific Markets, advertised in *WSJ,* 11/20/00.

If there is a job code in an announcement or advertisement, be sure to feature it in a similar fashion. Companies use these codes to route résumés and track responses, so make it easy for them:

Attn: Mr. Clyde Anthony Watkins, Director, Human Resources, Eastern Region

Re: Staff Accountant, ACC-27-NYT

## Cover Letters as an Accessory to Your Telephone

All of the above points will facilitate the routing of your résumé. Now let us consider what else to put in your cover letter. If you know for sure your contact is going to read your résumé, you can keep your letter exceedingly brief, e.g.:

Dear Mr. Witherspoon:

Here is my résumé, as you requested. I will call you by tomorrow afternoon to answer any preliminary questions you may have. In any case, I look forward to meeting with you on Thursday at nine o'clock. Meanwhile, I hope you are feeling better. I had a similar travel experience in Nigeria, but we can talk about that when we meet.

Short letters are usually appropriate for referral contacts as well.

Dear Charles:

As you requested, I have enclosed a few copies of my résumé for you to forward to potentially interested parties in Hong Kong. I appreciate your assistance, and I'll call you next week to follow up.

Because of the brevity of this type of cover letter, it can look terribly small way out in the middle of a piece of 8½-by-11-inch paper. It is a good idea to get some monarch-sized paper of the same weight and texture as your résumé for short letters. If that is not possible, just make your own. When you print your résumé, have them cut some of the paper to 7¼-by-10½ inches, or cut it yourself on a paper cutter. Do not cut across the watermark.

The proper protocol is to staple your résumé together, if it is more than one page, and to paperclip the cover letter to the résumé. I prefer gold-colored paperclips as a nice detail. Even when using monarch-sized paper, I would always type the cover letter. Handwritten letters communicate either intimacy or laziness, and neither is appropriate prior to your first meeting.

Whenever possible, you should use the telephone so forcefully that these short cover letters are sufficient. Not everybody is comfortable being a salesperson for themselves, however. If this is true of you, then your cover letters must do the selling for you.

## Cover Letters that Sell Résumés

If your letter is going to someone who is not obligated to read your résumé, you will need a traditional cover letter, a sales pitch for you and your résumé. These full-bodied cover letters have three functional parts.

➤ Introduction

➤ Rationale, or "pitch"

➤ Call to action

In your introduction, you say why you are writing. Specify the job or functional area in which you are interested and, of course, drop any names or referral sources right away. Some examples of introductory paragraphs are listed in the sections above.

Remember to lower the ante. Mention that you would like to "discuss possibilities," or "explore the potential for mutual interest." Do not say anything like "I'll be the best account executive you ever had on your team!"

In the main body of your letter, you *try to set yourself apart from other applicants.* You try to impress your reader with your accomplishments and talents. You can give a logical rationale for your candidacy or some type of sales pitch for yourself based on the quality of your experience and accomplishments.

If possible, relate your strengths to the requirements of the position and always gloss over or omit reference to any weaknesses. For example, if the ad specifies "college grads only" and you have no degree, focus on your skills, accomplishments, aggressive sales approach, whatever, but do not mention education at all. The cover letter is no place for excuses or negative points.

Be cautious of boasting that you know a lot about your potential employer's business, and avoid statements like "I know I would be a valuable asset to your business." If you have not interviewed for the position yet, that is a bit presumptuous, don't you think? We will look at some successful examples in a moment.

In the "call to action" you tell the reader what you want to happen next. Most cover letters, even from very savvy business leaders, lack a definitive call to action. This is the biggest mistake you could make. You must tell the reader what to do next, or suffer the consequences—usually the sorting stack or the black hole.

The number one way to avoid these consequences is to avoid them in advance, by proper use of your telephone. Other techniques all depend on the call to action in your cover letter.

The most effective call-to-action technique is that of telling your reader you will be calling soon, and soon means very soon. Contacts will read your résumé with greater interest and try to remember your name, *all subconsciously,* because they know you'll be calling. Remember your end-of-the-next-business-day time limit. Your call is going to have maximum impact during the first twenty-four hours after your material lands on your target's desk. You also will have more impact if you can say precisely when you will call. Here is a good example:

> I will call you on Tuesday at ten o'clock to follow up on this mailing. You can count on me to be prompt. I look forward to our conversation.

Needless to say, if you say you will call and you do not, your candidacy is much worse off than if you do not make such a promise in the first place. If you are someone who can't be sure to place a call precisely at 9:59 A.M., for example, then promise to make the call "on Tuesday before noon" or "before Wednesday of next week."

A weaker technique, but perhaps more comfortable for you, is to tell them to call you. It sounds simple, but it makes a difference. "Please call me to discuss this further." Without a line like this, without a call to action, your résumé is just one more piece of junk mail to be sorted and forgotten.

## Samples

In all of the following samples, look for the three key functional parts of a cover letter than sells:

- ➤ Introduction
- ➤ Rationale, or "pitch"
- ➤ Call to action

I prefer a cover letter that makes an argument, that in some way gives a rationale for your candidacy. The following letter had a phenomenal response rate for my candidate, even though she did not call and ask for interviews. The reason for her success was the outstanding rationale, which set her apart from the thousands of other, virtually identical candidates.

> Dear Hiring Partner:
>
> I am interested in opportunities to serve your firm as law clerk or extern this summer. I have several things to offer that may be of interest to you:
>
> 1. My high grades demonstrate my abilities and my desire to perform on your behalf. I have skills in research, writing, and case control. I take my assignments very seriously.

2. Although I am a first-year student, I already have paralegal and legal editing experience. I can be productive without any initial "break-in" period.

3. I speak conversational Japanese. If you do any work with native speakers of Japanese, I could be of benefit. Also, I know Japanese business protocol, which is just as important as the actual language.

I am interested in an opportunity to work closely with talented attorneys. I can offer detailed legal skills in support of their activities, accuracy, and a knowledge of my own limitations.

Please call me at your convenience to discuss this further. It would be a pleasure and an honor to be associated with your firm this summer.

Respectfully yours,

A. Winning Candidate

The following letter is in a style favored by fast-track professionals. It will work with any background with easily quantified, bottom-line accomplishments. The main body of the letter is a big pitch for the candidate; it *sells* the reader on the candidate's expertise. This particular letter targets a search firm but could easily be modified to target the head of sales for a company.

Dear Placement Specialist:

I have over 15 years of increasing responsibility as a sales rep and sales manager in the food-service industry. If you have any clients seeking someone with this type of background, perhaps you will be interested in these accomplishments:

- Increased volume by 217 percent for an established company. This was the result of a revitalization of sales efforts. No gimmicks—just hard, smart work.

- Introduced new product to 30,000 pounds in sales in first 90 days, more than 15 times our original target!

- Established sales programs for a new company resulting in 15,000 cases sold in first eight months.

- Earned *National* Salesman of the Year award in second year with McCormick & Company.

- Trained in sales and marketing with Procter & Gamble.

The above shows a top performer. For additional detail, I have provided the attached résumé for your review. You will see that I have management skills, endurance, and a desire for continued career challenge.

My present company is very happy with my performance, but it has gone through two mergers in the last six months. My position certainly seems to be secure, but I feel it is time for a wise man to consider his options.

If you have anything of interest to discuss, call me at your earliest convenience. I look forward to speaking with you soon.

Sincerely,

A. Strong Candidate

Whenever you write to a headhunter, demonstrate that you understand how the search business works. Ask for a referral to a client, not a lead on a job. Remember that you are in fact the commodity in this equation. Use lines like this: "Perhaps your timely introduction could be of benefit to all concerned" or "I should think that any of your clients who are in need of reducing their lead time from R&D to full commercialization would be interested in my accomplishments in this area."

Also, whenever writing to a headhunter, put this line in the letter: "Of course it is understood that you will not forward my material to any employer without discussing the specific opportunity with me first." Otherwise, you may find your résumé everywhere, like so much confetti falling over a Manhattan parade.

Although employment agencies welcome calls and visits from candidates, true headhunters do not. There's no need to call headhunters that don't know you or your best friend. For more on this, be sure to read John Lucht's *Rites of Passage.*

Broadcast cover letters are used for horizontal penetration of a large number of companies. For example, you might use one if you wish to sell your expertise in doing conversions from computer system A to the new, improved computer system B. If you can get a list of all companies who use system A, you can send them a broadcast cover letter with your résumé, to alert them to your service.

Of course, calling these same companies and establishing some sort of phone dialogue will be much more effective than just sending out letters.

Here is a broadcast cover letter for a mortgage banking specialist who specializes in cleaning up underperforming real estate portfolios.

Dear (Mr. or Ms. Regional Bank or S&L president or CEO):

As we discussed on the phone, my expertise spans most existing types of mortgage instruments: fixed-rate, ARM, CPM, GEM, and Wrap agreements. I have strong experience with GNMA and FNMA requirements, as well as specialized experience with the FSLIC.

From the attached you can see that my greatest strength is obviously project management for (1) quality assurance reviews of loan portfolios and various risk management studies, (2) due diligence related to the buying and selling of loans on the secondary market, (3) reconstruction of loan activity, (4) computer and operations conversions and mergers, (5) design and placement of quality assurance measures, and (6) staff training and the creation of a quality-oriented atmosphere.

In addition to project work, I can be available to serve as an interim manager or supervisor as needed.

I will be calling you on Wednesday before noon to follow up on this mailing, to discuss your own needs, and to see if you have any questions. Also, I can update you on recent projects, as this area of banking continues to be very exciting from an operational point of view.

Thank you for your interest.

Most sincerely,

A. Financial Savior

Broadcast letters can also be used by recent college graduates when they have a fairly well-defined employment target. Again, the letter is used to achieve horizontal penetration of a large volume of employers and must be **preceded by and followed with a telephone call** in order to get a positive response.

> Dear (Mr. or Ms. Employer):
>
> I am a recent graduate of the University of Illinois bachelor's program in architecture, including one year of study abroad at l'Ecole d'Architecture et de l'Urbanisme in Versailles.
>
> It is my desire to begin *in any capacity* with a prominent firm. I am eager to work with some talented designers, and you will see that I have a solid base of skills to contribute. I have autocad training, and my drafting, drawing, and rendering skills are sufficient to make immediate contributions to your projects. I am serious about my career, and I am sure you will find my skills and my professional attitude are in line with your high standards.
>
> I am seeking to join a firm that will offer me ongoing challenge and opportunity. My résumé details some of my technical skills, but you cannot tell whether you will be interested in me as a permanent employee until you see my portfolio. I think you will find the work of interest, and it will only take a moment to review the portfolio with you.
>
> In order to see if we have a mutual interest, I will be calling you on Thursday before noon. You can count on me to be prompt. It would be my pleasure to be available for a brief meeting at your convenience.
>
> Respectfully,
>
> A. Fine Candidate

When applying for a specific opening, you can tailor your entire presentation to keys in the announcement or advertisement. Do not use a point-by-point response, as this will only highlight your shortcomings. Giving a point-by-point presentation also makes it very easy for the employer to compare your background with others who respond using a similarly structured letter. Instead, read the announcement carefully and see what hints and subtleties you should address. There will be many, many candidates who have the minimum qualifications. You want to be the candidate who answers the employer's unstated but implied concerns.

Develop a prose presentation of your strengths relative to the needs of your target. The bigger the job, the longer your letter can be. The following letter won an interview at odds in excess of a hundred to one, even though my candidate was in Kansas and the targeted reader was a Los Angeles-based personnel consulting firm acting as a screen for the City of Irvine, California.

> Dear Mr. Donaldson:
>
> I was interested to come across your advertisement in *JobBANK* for manager of cultural affairs for the City of Irvine, California. I have been seeking an opportunity such as this, and I think you will find that I might fit your job description. I have enclosed my résumé for your review.

My background is in city planning and arts administration, which has proved to be an extremely effective combination. I believe my skills, abilities and accomplishments are represented, albeit briefly, on the enclosed materials.

In checking my background you will find that I have succeeded in two different but equally important areas: providing effective leadership, direction, and management and making the arts fun and participatory for a wide range of constituents, from public school students to major benefactors. It is difficult to show "feel good" accomplishments, but you will note that throughout my career I have been able to marshal the support, cooperation, and enthusiasm of an incredibly diverse set of peers and colleagues.

I feel that I have been instrumental in generating long-term benefit for the organizations which I have served, and that benefit can best be summarized as (1) increased financial support, (2) increased public support, and (3) increased organizational efficiency.

I already have good friends in Southern California, and relocation to the area would be welcome. This position is of great interest to me. I think that your client, the City of Irvine, might be interested in my candidacy as well. Perhaps your introduction would be beneficial to all concerned.

Thank you for your attention to these materials, and I'll be calling you very soon to see if you have any questions and to discuss your selection process.

Yours sincerely,

A. Fantastic Candidate

When there is no opening, it is usually a good idea to acknowledge this. Use lines like "I would like to discuss career opportunities with your representative" or, if you want to have an informal or informational interview, "I am not applying for a particular position at this time; I am just interested in discussing possibilities. I'll be calling you soon to see if we can arrange a meeting at your convenience."

Key words to drop into any cover letter are *fit* and *mutual interest.* When you manage your career right, you will be interviewing your contact companies just as closely as they will be interviewing you. The more you realize and act on this, the more respect you will get from your interviewers, and the better "fit" and the greater "mutual interest" you will find.

You do not have to mention why you are leaving your current employer, but if you do, it should be stated in a way that bolsters your candidacy: "My future certainly would be secure with my current employer, but I am not just interested in security. To be honest with you, they do not have any major new projects planned for me, and I would like a new challenge."

If for any reason you left your last employer under a cloud, go back and negotiate exactly what they will say about you as a reference. This is easier than you think. Nobody wants litigation over your discharge, and the awards escalate rapidly if malice can be shown on the part of the employer. Incidentally, if you want to sue your current or former employer, *get a new job first.* Then sue.

The following two pages show cover letters appropriately laid out in a conservative, business letter format. The first is a targeted application for a management candidate; the second is a broadcast letter for a recent college graduate. Note the strong impression conveyed of the candidates' personalities and work philosophies.

## Tara Lynn Johnson

4 White Street, Apt. 5B
New York, New York, 10013

Personal e-mail: taralynn@netcom.com
Office phone/voicemail: (212) 555-2620
Residence phone/message: (212) 555-3134

October 18, 2000

Attn: **Human Resources,** Department DK
Re: Position for **Collection Manager,** Tuesday *Wall Street Journal*, 10/16/2000

Dean Witter Reynolds, Inc.
Tower Office, 2 WTC, 73rd Floor
New York, New York 10048

Dear Placement Specialist:

I was very interested to see your advertisement for a collections manager. I have long been interested in your company, and this is a position in which I believe I could excel on your behalf. I am enclosing my résumé for your consideration.

As you can see from my résumé I have advanced accounting and collections experience for a financial services company. My experience spans multistate collection of receivables ranging from small amounts up to $1 million. My authority includes direct negotiation and settlement of receivables, and I work with the company's special counsel for collections on cases as warranted. My greatest collection success, however, has been more organizational in nature: (1) training and motivating collections staff, and (2) making contributions to policy and procedure that have drastically reduced our need to pursue receivables in the first place.

Other strengths include (1) management of accounting staff, (2) design of reporting formats, (3) cash management and cash flow control, (4) operations analysis and contributions to design of IT in association with programmers/analysts, and (5) management of human resources administration. These skills may not apply directly to your position, but my experience in these areas will certainly contribute to my ability to perform.

My orientation is toward preventing problems at the point of origination, but I can be quite creative, persistent, and articulate in both logical and persuasive argument to achieve collections goals.

I hope my background will warrant an interview to discuss this further. Please call me. My office is not far from yours, and I would be happy to meet with you at your convenience to see if we can establish a mutual interest.

Yours sincerely,

*Tara Lynn Johnson*
Tara Lynn Johnson

Enclosure: résumé
Salary: negotiable

/tj

**Margaret Knobloch**

6468 Williams Street
Omaha, Nebraska 68106

Telephone/Message
(402) 555-1707

June 10, 2001

Ms. Lisa Dale Norton
Vice President, Human Resources
U.S. West
110 South 19th Street
Omaha, Nebraska 68106

Dear Ms. Norton:

I am interested in having a short, face-to-face talk with you about
opportunities in telecommunications.

As you can see from the attached, I am a recent college graduate with a
strong liberal arts education. My greatest strengths would have to be my
oral and written communication skills. I am a self-starter. I applied for
and thoroughly enjoyed a year abroad, held several elected offices in
school, and started a local chapter of a national sorority. I have all
the routine office skills, as well as strong organizational abilities as
demonstrated in the internships listed on my résumé.

I would be interested in a customer-service position or other position
involving direct customer contact. Since there are many ways in which I
could serve you, I would like to explore that in a personal meeting.

Even if you don't anticipate any openings, a moment of your time would be
appreciated. I'd like to hear what ideas you may have for me.

Thank you so much for your attention. I'll be calling you shortly to see
if we can arrange a time to get together.

Yours sincerely,

*Margaret Knobloch*

Margaret Knobloch

Enclosure: Résumé.
/mk

## Customize Your Letters

Anyone at the management level who does not write individual, customized letters is not serious about her job search. Even though you will soon develop a handful of letters that you modify only slightly to use over and over again, each one must be individually typed or word-processed and completely free of errors. The typeface on the letter does not have to match the typeface of the résumé. As a matter of act, a different face confirms the personalized nature of the letter.

If you are not a management candidate, however, there is a shortcut that will work in an emergency. I use this technique with clients who do not have a computer, or even a typewriter, and who simply do not have enough money to manage a proper job search. I write a slightly vague cover letter addressed to the "Prospective Employer," with headings at the top for the date and address. The candidate fills in the date and address neatly by hand.

If the candidate is responding to a newspaper advertisement, she cuts the ad out and tapes it onto the top of her cover letter (in addition to writing in the data and addressee by hand). This way the company knows what position she is applying for, and how to route her résumé. Remember, the easier it is to route your résumé, the more likely it will be read by someone who is in a position to give you a job.

The following cover letter demonstrates this generic cover letter approach. This cover letter won the candidate a good position with a law firm, even though she had no legal background. A generic cover letter will not work for a management candidate, but in an emergency it is far better than no cover letter at all.

---

**Sandy McKie**

1602 Lancaster Lane
Baltimore Maryland 21205
(301) 555-9348

Date: Jan. 10, 2000

Attn: Valerie Adams

Dear Prospective Employer:

**Case Assistant**

Smart, well org, able to work indpndtly? Track/control complex details of financial lit. 2 yrs. F/T legal exp., exc. writing skills req. NY firm expanding Balt. Great potential. Res. to Valerie Adams, P.O. 12586, Balt., 21210

In the interest of exploring employment opportunities within your organization, I have enclose a copy of my résumé briefly describing my qualifications and credentials.

As my résumé indicates, I have a solid background in administrative services. I have been involved at the supervisory level in the full spectrum of support activities, from directing secretarial staff to administering accounting and billing operations. I have a reputation for dedication and quality performance. I am willing to give an assignment whatever it takes to bring it to fruitful completion.

Please consider me a serious candidate for any administrative position for which I may be qualified. I would like to meet with you to discuss your needs and how I may best be utilized to your success. Please contact me to arrange an interview at your convenience.

Thank you for your consideration. I look forward to our conversation.

Respectfully yours,

*Sandy McKie*

Sandy McKie

Encl: Résumé

For some candidates, writing letters can be an invitation to disaster. Résumés have a controlled and formulaic style. Cover letters do not, so they can reveal faults that résumés will naturally hide. Bad syntax can come flying out of nowhere. Bad thinking can rear its ugly head. Creative spelling can slip by in your hurry to get the letter in the mail. In general, if you have a good résumé, let it do its job. Keep your cover letter short and to the point, use the telephone, and keep your job search moving along.

If you have any reason to doubt your ability to turn out a large volume of perfect cover letters, you can make a utilitarian cover letter with just an introduction and a call to action. The following cover letter can be used over and over again, if you have a good résumé and the will to use your phone.

> Dear (Ms. or Mr. Next Employer):
>
> In the interest of exploring employment opportunities with you in the area of (you name it), I have enclosed my résumé briefly describing my qualifications and credentials.
>
> With my experience and background, I am confident that I can make a meaningful and lasting contribution to my next employer. I will be calling you soon to discuss this further, and to see if we can establish a mutual interest.
>
> Please keep my résumé handy, and I can answer any questions you may have when I call. Thank you for your attention, and I look forward to our conversation.
>
> Yours sincerely,
>
> (Your Name Here)

It's not art, but it'll definitely do the job.

Once again, do not respond to requests for salary history in a cover letter or any pre-interview communiqué.

## References

Do not provide your references until they are requested, but it is a good idea to know who you would like to use and ask their permission. I recommend that you send your résumé to your references in advance. This refreshes their memory of how great you are and allows you to prep them on what you want them to say.

Ideally, your references would be your immediate superiors in your last two or three jobs, preferably someone with direct knowledge of your daily job performance, not a distant CEO who was thrilled with your production figures but had no working knowledge of you.

Incidentally, if you are afraid to send your résumé to your old employers, then it may be inflated. You might want to tone it down to something you know they will endorse.

Peers and subordinates are useless references, as no one will believe them anyway. If you must, you can use vendors, suppliers, or clients of your current company while you are still employed.

Tailor your references to the particular application. For example, if your potential employer seems concerned about your financial skills, your first reference should be able to describe a financial problem you solved or financial project you managed.

If your job search takes a long time, rotate your references, and communicate often with them. The last thing you want is for one of them to become irritated and say to a potential employer, "Jeez, hasn't he gotten a job yet?"

It is not unreasonable to have a very smooth friend call your references, pretending to be a headhunter, and check them out.

A reference listing has the name, current title, current business address, and current daytime telephone number of your endorser. If your connection is not obvious, then state it in parentheses.

**Reference:**

Al Gore
President, United States
(Formerly vice president, United States, when I was a citizen there)
The White House
Washington, D.C. 20500
(202) 456-1414

# Go for It! This Is Your Life

## CHAPTER 17

The ability to switch jobs successfully is a talent like any other. It is a talent that can be learned by anybody and can be improved with practice and study. If you learn this talent well, then you will almost always love your job. Conversely, you will almost never hate your boss, you will be unlikely to feel that your salary is an insult, and you will seldom wonder "what if . . ." for very long before you do something about it.

In the modern job market, your first obligation is to your own career development. If you do not get promotions on a regular basis, then consider a move. If you are not happy, consider a move. My most ambitious clients tell me they expect a promotion every eighteen months or fewer. If they do not get one within that time frame, they will definitely begin the process of switching companies.

I am not recommending that you sacrifice the rest of your life for your career. On the contrary, I am recommending that you have whatever kind of career you want to complement your life as a whole. The principles in this book are sound. They will work to facilitate your career direction, whatever it may be. They can be translated into the non-profit sector, government service, or the creative arts.

Set your sights high, whatever that means for you. Go for it. This is your life. You are the boss.

Reprinted with permission

# Appendix: Annotated Bibliography of Career Books

## CHAPTER 18

## The Enemy of Action is Research!!!!

If you are ready to launch your job search, DO IT NOW and read these books later. Nobody ever learned to swim or play golf by reading a book. You can improve your game by reading these books, but they will only help if you are willing to get wet or slash a few divots first.

## Books on Job-Search and Career Advancement Strategies

Books in this section can help you hone a particular skill, such as interviewing or utilizing headhunters effectively. They can also provide far greater understanding of the job-search process than is available in this thin volume. However, you should know that the résumé material in some of these books is obsolete, in some cases dangerously obsolete. *Verbum sat sapienti est.* So, be sure to use only the more recently published and updated books or those listed that are dedicated to the topic for developing your résumé-writing skills. If some of the books you want are now out of print, and if you would like to check them out, go to your local library, find a local bookstore that will special order them, or check out Amazon Books or Advanced Book Exchange on the Web (www.amazon.com and www.abebooks.com, respectively) where they'll try their best to find them for you.

The original bible of the job-search process is certainly *What Color is Your Parachute?* by Richard Bolles. This book is revised annually, and anyone who is interested in changing careers, entering the job market, or reentering the job market should definitely read it. I read it every year and learn something new each time.

If you are a management or professional person pursuing the second, third, or higher rung of your career, I would recommend one of the more comprehensive books. At senior levels, I am fond of *Rites of Passage at $100,000+*, by John Lucht. It is one of the most refreshing books on the subject I have read in years, and it comes right from the heart of experience. A good companion guide would be my *Asher's Bible of Executive Résumés*. At more moderate levels, try *The Only Job Hunting Guide You'll Ever Need* or *The Complete Job-Search Handbook*, both satisfyingly comprehensive encyclopedias. Also good is *How to Get a Better Job in This Crazy World*, by the placement guru Robert Half. And now that the world has been taken over by computers, *The Electronic Job Search Revolution* is good for those who want to know how to use this revolution to their advantage in the job-search process.

➤ *The 2000 What Color is Your Parachute? A Practical Manual for Job-Hunters and Career-Changers*. Richard Nelson Bolles. Berkeley: Ten Speed Press, 1999.

➤ *The Complete Job-Search Handbook: All the Skills You Need to Get Any Job and Have a Good Time Doing it*. Howard Figler, Ph.D. New York: Henry Holt and Co., rev. ed., 1988.

➤ *The Electronic Job Search Revolution*. Joyce Lain Kennedy and Thomas J. Morrow. New York: John Wiley & Sons, 2nd ed., 1995.

➤ *How to Get a Better Job in This Crazy World*. Robert Half. New York: Signet, 1994.

➤ *The Only Job Hunting Guide You'll Ever Need: The Most Comprehensive Guide for Job Hunters and Career Switchers*. Kathryn and Ross Petras. New York: Poseidon Press, 1995.

➤ *Rites of Passage at $100,000+: The Insider's Guide to Absolutely Everything About Executive Job-Changing*. John Lucht. New York: Viceroy Press, 1993.

## How to Do Research on Companies

People who find this topic mysterious are usually the same people who have never set foot in the reference section of their city's library. The reference librarians are there to help you, and you can bet they will if you already know what you want to look for. The books in this section are a good place to start.

Also, if you are interested in a major corporation, call its investor relations department and tell them you are interested in investing in their company (which is true) or just say that you will soon have an appointment with someone in the company and you want to be informed for the meeting (which is also true). Ask for any general information and any financial information they may have. If the company does not have an investor relations department, ask for the corporate communications department or the public relations department.

Unless you are an accountant, analyst, or senior manager, do not worry too much about the financial information. You want to know what the company does, where it came from, and where it thinks it is going. The company's own material will tell you clearly. You can then ask yourself some questions: Is it going to be a high-growth corporation? Is it already there? Do you support the company's intentions and would you feel comfortable working there? If you still want to review the company's financials and understand them, first read Tracy's *How to Read a Financial Report.*

Also, it is a good idea to check *Who's Who* to see what information you can find on top officers. Maybe your interviewer is in there too—you never know.

Finally, check your local business press for articles in the last six months on the company in question, and check the national business press through the *Business Periodicals Index.*

## General Guides

➤ *The 100 Best Companies to Work for in America.* Robert Levering et al. New York: Plume, rev. ed., 1994.

➤ *150 Best Companies for Liberal Arts Graduates: Where to Get a Job in Tough Times.* Cheryl Woodruff and Greg Ptacek. New York: John Wiley & Sons, 1992.

➤ *Forbes' Top Companies: The Forbes Annual Review of Today's Leading Businesses.* Jonathan T. Davis, ed., et al. New York: Forbes, Inc., 1997.

➤ *Hoover's Handbook of Emerging Companies 1996.* Patrick J. Spain and James R. Talbot, eds. Austin, TX: The Reference Press, Inc., 1995.

➤ *How to Read a Financial Report.* John A. Tracy. New York: John Wiley & Sons, 4th ed., 1993.

➤ *The Job Seeker's Guide to 1000 Top Employers.* Jennifer Arnold Mast. Detroit: Visible Ink Press, 1993.

➤ *The Job Seeker's Guide to Socially Responsible Companies.* Katherine Jankowski. Detroit: Visible Ink Press, 1995.

➤ *Peterson's Hidden Job Market, 1998: 2000 High Growth Companies that Are Hiring at Four Times the National Average.* Karen Hansen, ed. Princeton, NJ: Peterson's Guides, 1997. (published annually)

## Periodicals

➤ *Business Periodicals Index.* Bronx: Wilson Publishing.

➤ *Directory of Corporate Affiliations.* Wilmette, IL: National Register Publishing Company.

➤ *Directories in Print.* Detroit: Gale Research.

➤ *Encyclopedia of Associations.* Detroit: Gale Research.

➤ *Encyclopedia of Business Information Sources.* Detroit: Gale Research. Biannual.

➤ *Guide to American Directories.* Coral Springs, FL: B. Klein Publications. Biannual.

➤ *National Directory of Addresses and Telephone Numbers.* Kirkland, WA: General information.

➤ *Reference Book of Corporate Management.* Parsippany, NJ: Dun & Bradstreet.

➤ *Standard Directory of Advertisers* (by product and location). Wilmette, IL: National Register Publishing Company.

➤ *Standard & Poor's Register of Corporations, Directors, & Executives.* New York: Standard & Poor.

➤ *State Manufacturing Directories.* Vary by state, but every state has one.

➤ *Thomas' Register of American Manufacturers.* New York: Thomas Publishing.

➤ *Who's Who in America.* Wilmette, IL: Marquis Who's Who.

➤ *Who's Who in Finance & Industry.* Wilmette, IL: Marquis Who's Who.

➤ *Yellow Pages.* Note: Some airports and libraries have telephone directories from every major U.S. city.

### Specific Guides (a few examples; see the business section of your local library for more)

➤ *1998–1999 National Directory of Legal Employers.* Chicago: Harcourt Brace.

➤ *Aerospace Companies.* Greenwich, CT: DMS, Inc.

➤ *Biotechnology Industry Guide.* Research Triangle Park, NC: Institute for Biotechnology Information, LLC.

➤ *Chemical Industry Corporate Profiles.* New York: Schnell Publishing.

➤ *Data Sources—The Comprehensive Guide to the Information Processing Industry.* New York: Ziff-Davis.

➤ *Hoover's Guide to Computer Companies.* Austin, TX: Hoover's Business Press.

➤ *Insurance Almanac.* Englewood, NJ: Underwriter Printing and Publishing.

➤ *Rand McNally International Bankers Directory.* Chicago: Rand McNally.

➤ *World Chamber of Commerce Directory.* Loveland, CO: World Chamber of Commerce Directory.

➤ *World Directory of Pharmaceutical Manufacturers.* London: IMS World Publications.

And so on, ad infinitum.

➤ ➤

Donald Asher is one of America's premiere career management gurus. He runs an executive coaching business from San Francisco, lectures from coast to coast on careers and higher education, consults to corporations on staffing transition and executive development issues, and is a frequent guest on radio and television. The contents of this book are the result of over a decade of service to fast-track careerists, the motivated, highly successful individuals who continue to double their income throughout their careers. If you are interested in developing the fast-track habits of your employees, if you want a dynamic speaker to address the next meeting of your trade group or professional association, then call Asher Associates today. Asher Associates, San Francisco, (415) 543-7130.

# Index

Page numbers followed by *ex* refer to example résumé.

abbreviations, 8, 9
academic style, 78, 84–85 ex
accomplishments, 5–6, 30, 31–33
accountant/bookkeeper, 67 ex
account manager, 68 ex
account relations, 63 ex
acronyms, 8, 9
activities, 46
actor style, 78, 87 ex
additional data on résumé, 46–49
"additional education" section, 46, 52
"additional" section, 48
administrative assistant, 67 ex, 93 ex
advertising style, 78, 86 ex
affiliations, 46
appointments, confirming, 126–127
artist bio, 78, 89 ex
artist style, 78, 88 ex

background check, 44, 52
banking, manager, job listings, 35 ex
blind box ads, 135–136
bullets, 14
business press, 119, 121, 153
buyer, 99101 ex

CAD specialist, 70 ex
call—write—call, 122–124, 142
career-oriented Web sites, 103–105
career-search message board, 104
cat, Ernie, 79, 94 ex
chronological career history, 23
chronological style, 11–12
civil/structural engineer job listing, 37 ex
clerical, 75 ex
clinical psychologist profile, 28 ex
cold contacts, 118–119
college placement offices, 120
community service, 46
company guides, 153
company name, disguising, 30
compensation package, total, 131
computer and high-tech job- search Web sites, 110–111
conservative presentation, 53
consultant style job listing, 37–38 ex
consultant vita, 78–79, 90 ex
consulting and unemployment periods, 38
controlling reader's eye, 12–14
corporate communications, 69 ex
corporation
    general and financial information, 152–153
    officers, information on, 153
coursework, 45

cover letter
    addressed to particular person, 135, 136
    broadcast, 141–142
        recent graduate, 142, 143, 145 ex
        specialty, 141 ex
    call to action, 137, 140–143 ex, 144–145 ex
    conservative, business letter format, 143, 144–145 ex
    critical information in, 135
    customizing, 146
    emergency shortcut, 146
    excuses, negativity, boasting in, 138
    format, 146
    from different city, 142–143
    functional parts, 138–139
    generic, 146
    heading, 137
    introduction 136–137 ex, 139–142 ex, 144–145 ex
    management candidate, 143, 144–145 ex
    purpose, 135
    rationale or pitch, 139–140
    reusable, 146
    routing, 135–137, 146
    salary comments in, 125
    solicited, 136–137
    telephone follow-up, 139
    why leaving current employer in, 143
credentials, 46
curriculum vitae style, 78, 84–85 ex

database management, 56 ex
degrees, advanced, 44
dental hygienist profile, 27 ex
design development, 64 ex
directories, 153–154
drafting, 64 ex
driver job listings, 42 ex
driver training, 65 ex

education
    dates, 51
    listings, 43–46
        recent college graduate, 45
    nonexistent, 44
    omitting some, 46
electronic résumés, 95–98, 99–101 ex
    format, 97
e-mail, 21
employer
    current, 119
    former, talking about, 125
    point of view, 16, 24, 29, 30, 34, 46, 52
    suing, 143
    to contact in job search, 117
employment, continuous, 41
employment agencies, 120, 141
employment dates, 30
    deemphasizing, 41
    obfuscating, 41–42
employment history, 4
encompassing statement, 52
engineer style job listing, 37–38 ex
engineer, 71 ex
entry level, 26

envelopes, 53
ethnic identity, 47
exaggerating grossly, 4
examples, using, 53
executive assistant, job listing, 35–36
executive job-search Web sites, 111–113
experience, 29–42
   divided into categories, 30
   extraneous data in section, 30
   getting, 40
   headings for, 29
   listing, 25, 39–40
   non-job, 25, 29, 39–40
   older, 52
expertise, describing, 24
extra copies at interview, 4

F & B operations, 73 ex
fax, 13, 125
federal job-search Web sites, 114
field or company contacts, 118
film job style, 78, 88 ex
finance style, 77–78, 82–83 ex
financial analysis, 55 ex
follow-up details, tracking, 127–129, 130
follow-up letter, 127
food server job listing, 38 ex
format, 6, 12–14
   numbers, 7
functional style, 11–12, 79, 93 ex

gender, identifying, 19–20
general contracting, 66 ex
goals, achieving with résumé, 4
goals, deciding before interview, 5
guides to specific industries, 154

headhunters, 120, 141
heading, 19–21, 22 ex
   cover letter, 137
   placement, 14
hidden job market, 121
high school diploma, 46
hiring authorities, 116
hiring authorities, routing to, 23
hiring cycle, 126
hiring decision, justifying, 3, 4
hiring process, asking about, 127
hobbies, 47–48
home page, 98
homophobia, 47
hospitality IT profile, 26 ex
HTML résumés, 95–98, 101 ex
human resources, 58 ex
human resources directors, 120
hyperlinks, 97, 98

ideal candidate, envisioning, 17
industry press, 119, 121, 153
industry styles, 77–79, 80–94 ex
informational interview, 121–122
insider's language, 8, 9
interest, information listed in order of, 24, 29, 30, 34, 46, 52
Internet
   résumé-posting on, 119
   Web sites, 103–114, 119
Internet résumés, 25, 95–98, 101 ex

interview
   asking for, 123
   getting, 3, 121–127
   notes on, 127
   objections to granting, 123–124
   résumé living up to, 4
interviewer's memory, overwhelming with résumé, 4
investment analysis, 55 ex
investor relations department, 152
IS generalist, 56 ex

jargon, 8, 9
job announcement, hints and subtleties in, 142
job club, 129
job listings, 34–42, 34–39 ex, 42 ex
   common problems, 38–42
   components 34
   omissions in, 41–42
   out of chronological order, 41
   regrouped under subheadings, 41
job search
   as new job, 133
   clothes, 115
   job hunting guides, 151–152
   increasing action, 123–124
   organizing and managing, 127–129
   protocol, 125
   psychology, 132–133
   resources, 115
   strategies, 115
   timing, 124–125, 126
job-search Web sites, general, 103110
job-search weekly report, 130
job section subheadings, 30
job targeting, 16
job titles, 30

languages, 46, 48
lead list, building, 116–121
legal style, 77, 80–81 ex
length, electronic résumé, 96
liberal arts education, 145
library, public, 119, 152
licenses, 46
life science job-search Web sites, 113–114
lying, 4, 6, 44
   consequences of, 6, 41

mailing address, 21–22
management, administrative, profile, 26 ex
manager, 57 ex, 60 ex, 62 ex, 68 ex, 93 ex
manager, office. *See* office manager
marketing, 63 ex, 72 ex
marketing consultant job listing, 38
mechanical designer, 70 ex
medical style, 78, 84–85 ex
merchandiser, 99–101 ex
military experience, 40–41
military experience job listing, 40 ex
modeling style, 78, 87 ex
mortgage banking profile, 27 ex
multiple addresses, 21, 22
musician style, 78, 88 ex

network controller profile, 27 ex
networking, telephone, 116–118, 121

new applications
   weekly goals, 128–129, 130
new business development, 57 ex, 72 ex
newspapers, 120–121
nickname, 19

offers, firm, 129
office, general, 75 ex
office manager, 93 ex
office manager profile, 26 ex
off the market, 132
omissions, 34, 41–42, 51, 79
operations analysis, 71 ex
overselling yourself, 132

page breaks, numbers and headings, 96
paper, 53, 127, 138
people to contact in job search, 117
periodicals, 119, 121, 153
personal mailing, 136
personal section
   American omissions, 48
   international inclusions, 48–49
photocopying, 53
physical science job-search Web sites, 113, 114
picture, 98
point of view, 16, 24, 29, 30, 34, 46, 52
politics, 47
portfolio, 49
postage, 53
postal service L.S.M. operator job listing, 39 ex
prejudices, subconscious, 51
prep school, 46
president, manufacturing company, job listing, 36–37 ex
president, student union, experience listing, 39 ex
printing, 52, 53
prior section, 52
production, 52–53
profile, 23–26, 26–28 ex
   heading for, 24
   in cover letter, 52
   when to use, 52
promotional work, 72 ex
promotions, regular, 149
psychology of job search, 132–133
publication list, 49
public relations, 69 ex
public relations department, 152
punch ending, 48
punctuality, 125

quantities, exact, 31

real estate lending, 61 ex
real estate profile, 27 ex
recent college graduate
   education listings, 45
   no work history, 92 ex
receptionist, job listing, 34 ex
reference librarian, 119, 152
references, 49, 147–148, 148 ex
   negotiating with former employers, 143
regional guides, 119
remodeling, 66 ex
research associate, chemistry, experience listing, 40 ex
research on companies, 152
restaurant manager job listing, 36 ex

restoration, historical, 66 ex
résumé, functions of, 3
résumé and cover letter, assembling, 138
résumé-posting Web sites, 103, 106–114
résumé service, 52, 53
routing, 23, 135–137, 146
rules, breaking, 5
rules of résumé writing, 5–6

sailing team captain, experience listing, 40 ex
salary, 31, 125, 147
salary negotiations, 129, 131–132
sales, 63 ex, 68 ex, 72 ex
   floor covering, profile, 28 ex
sales management, 57 ex, 68 ex
sales rep, envisioning ideal, 17
scannable résumés, 25, 95–98, 99–100 ex
scanning, preparing résumé for, 96–97
school projects, 45
science job-search Web sites, 113–114
scientific style, 78, 84–85 ex
search engines, 3, 95–96
search tools, 95
secretary, 75 ex, 93 ex
self-employment, downplaying, 40
shortening résumé, 51
skills, 25, 47
small business manager, 60 ex
speaker's vita, 78–79, 90 ex
staff & operations management, 62 ex
state employment development departments, 120
store management, 57 ex
strengths, 25, 44
student activities and experience, 39–40
styles, 11–12
   industry, 77–79, 80–94 ex
systems administration, 56 ex

technical résumés, 25
telecommunications, cover letter, 145 ex
telephone
   before writing cover letter, 135
   calls, random, 136
   calls to targeted companies, 123–124
text blocks, 14
thank-you note, 127
"throw-out factors," 47, 51
trade press, 119, 121, 153
training, staff, 71 ex
transcripts, 49
travel experiences, 48
trucking safety, 65 ex
truth, telling best side of, 32
TV job style, 78, 88 ex
typesetting, 15
type styles, 12–13

underlining, 12–13
unsolicited résumés, 3

watermark, 53
Web sites
   companies' own, 119
   job search, 103–114
   want ads on, 119
word processing, 15, 52, 75 ex
writing samples, 49

# Also by Donald Asher

### Asher's Bible of Executive Résumés & How to Write Them

The largest compendium of executive résumés ever published for the general public, with everything you need to know, including hints on upgrading your current job, getting headhunted, and more.

### The Foolproof Job-Search Workbook

Just open this book up and follow the instructions, and you will get job offers . . . guaranteed. The systematic, proven methodology in this book will enable you to build an effective job-hunting network, get the offers you want, and the salary you deserve. If not, you can just return the filled-in workbook to the publisher and receive a full refund. No one has had to take us up on it yet!

### Graduate Admissions Essays—What Works, What Doesn't, and Why

The definitive book on writing a unique, innovative essay that will get any student noticed by even the most exacting admissions committees.

# . . . And More Help for the Job Hunter

### What Color Is Your Parachute? by Richard N. Bolles

This classic in the career field is substantially revised and updated every year. Practical advice, step-by-step exercises, and a warm, human tone make it *the* guide for job hunters and career changers. "The giant in the field"—*New York Times*

### Dynamic Cover Letters, Revised, by Katherine Hansen and Randall Hansen

Completely new letters help the job seeker create the kind of cover letter that will get the resume read and virtually guarantee an interview.

### 200 Letters for Job Hunters, Revised, by William S. Frank

The standard resource for people who need letters of all types—from campaign to follow-up—for the job search.

### Negotiating Your Salary: How to Make $1000 a Minute, by Jack Chapman

This example-packed step-by-step manual explains exactly what to say and do to get the best possible compensation.

**TEN SPEED PRESS**
P.O. Box 7123
Berkeley, California 94707
1-800-841-BOOK
order@tenspeed.com
www.tenspeed.com